The Quakers

*Cover: The old Friends Meeting House
in King Street, Melksham*

Twelve Quakers quite ſtill.

From an early eighteenth century woodcut: Granny, fourth from left of the second row wears the old mid-seventeenth century steeple hat. Mamma, second from left in the same row, wears the later seventeenth century hood but daughter (on her right) has a fashionable little eighteenth century tricorne. All the men wear Quaker broadbrims, except the man with crossed legs in the second row, who wears the straight-brimmed hat which preceded it. Some men are wearing seventeenth century Puritan collars but all thre women have eighteenth century tuckers.

(Adapted from notes by the late Beatrice Saxon Snell)

The Quakers of Melksham
1669 - 1950

Harold Fassnidge

with illustrations by
Jane Townesend

Published in 1992 by
Bradford on Avon Friends

8 ST MARGARET'S HILL
BRADFORD ON AVON
WILTS BA15 1DP

Design and typesetting by
Ex Libris Press
1 The Shambles
Bradford on Avon
Wiltshire

Cover printed by
Shires Press, Trowbridge
Printed and bound in Great Britain by
Dotesios Ltd., Trowbridge

ISBN 0 9519433 0 8

F 98.24

Harold Fassnidge has also written a history of Bradford on
Avon : *Bradford on Avon: Past and Present* (Ex Libris Press: 1988)
and co-edited with Peter Maundrell *Bradford on Avon: A Pic-
torial Record* (published in 1983 by Wiltshire Library and Museum Service)

CONTENTS

ACKNOWLEDGEMENTS

I am grateful to Mary Bell of Bradford on Avon, Walter Birmingham of Shaftesbury, Dr. Jonathan Brown of Reading University, Dr. and Mrs. Ian Cardy of Melksham, Pamela Coleman, librarian of the Wiltshire Archaeological and Natural History Society, Barbara and Robert Harvey of Winsley, Bradford of Avon, Edward Milligan, formerly librarian at Friends House, London, John Poulson of Corsham, Pamela Slocombe, of Wiltshire Buildings Record, and Malcolm Thomas, librarian at Friends House, London. I am especially grateful to Margery Still for her checking of my typescript and constructive criticism.

Ever helpful have been the Wiltshire Record Office, the Local Studies Section of the Wiltshire Library and Museum Service and the library at Friends House.

I would also like to thank Roger Jones, (Ex Libris Press), for his patience, attention to detail and general professionalism in seeing the job through from raw manuscript to finished book.

Publication was facilitated by the Edward Cadbury Charitable Trust, the Edith M. Ellis 1985 Charitable Trust, the Joseph Rowntree Charitable Trust and the C.B. and H.H. Taylor Trust.

The illustrations on pages 34, 92, 104, 105, 107, 109, 110, 111 and 112 are reproduced by courtesy of the library of Friends House, London and those on pages 97 and 98 by courtesy of the Institute of Agricultural History amd Rural Life of the University of Reading.

FOREWORD

My sources have been largely the minute-books and other documents of the Wiltshire Meetings of the Religious Society of Friends in Wiltshire Record Office at Trowbridge where all known records belonging to the North Somerset and Wiltshire Quaker Monthly Meeting are deposited. My study of the earliest minute books (*viz* up to 1730) was facilitated by the careful transcripts and notes of the late Misses Beatrice and Nina Saxon Snell of Reading Monthly Meeting of the Religious Society of Friends, copies of which are on open shelves in the Record Office.

Where information derives from minute-books the source is readily identified by the date given in the text. The relevant minute-books for the present purposes are:

Wiltshire Quarterly Meeting 1678-1785
Chippenham Monthly Meeting 1669-1775
Charlcote Monthly Meeting 1709-1775
Lavington (or Southern) Monthly Meeting 1704-1775
Wiltshire Monthly Meeting 1775-1876
Wiltshire Monthly Meeting of Women Friends 1798-1818
North Somerset and Wiltshire Monthly Meeting from 1876

Minutes of London Yearly Meeting (the annual meeting of Friends in England, Scotland and Wales) are kept at Friends House in London.

References to material other than minutes are furnished in the usual way.

As annexes I have included material not necessarily bearing directly on Melksham Meeting itself but likely to be of general interest in its context. The names, occupations and residence of Quaker trustees at Appendix H may be of interest to family historians but should not be taken as exhaustive; there are many more Quaker deeds and documents in the Wiltshire Record Office than I have needed for the present work.

Quakerism spread rapidly throughout the county in the second half of the seventeenth century and declined almost equally rapidly in the eighteenth. The decline continued into the nineteenth and twentieth centuries. By 1827 only three (Calne, Melksham and Salisbury) remained of the nineteen Quaker places of worship registered under the Toleration Act of 1689. But meetings never ceased altogether and the second half of the present century has seen a modest revival. Today there are six viable Meetings (Bradford on Avon, Chippenham, Devizes, Marlborough, Salisbury and Swindon) with between them a total listed membership of some 200 or so. Melksham, the largest, most influential in its early days and longest continuously surviving Friends Meeting in the county has, however, so far failed to revive.

Harold Fassnidge
Bradford on Avon, 1992

1 THE MOVEMENT

Quakerism was born in the turbulent aftermath of the English Civil War. The date usually assigned is 1652. In December of that year the elements of organisation emerged when regular meetings were established in the East Riding of Yorkshire. Early adherents called themselves Friends in Truth; the term Society of Friends came into use about 1665. The term Quaker is a nickname based on a gibe. In 1650 Gervase Bennet, a justice of the peace, bidden by George Fox, the chief leader of the new movement, to tremble at the name of the Lord, derisively referred to him as "the quaker". The name stuck. I use the term Quaker equally with the term Friend throughout.

George Fox came of God-fearing parents. His father was a churchwarden at Fenny Drayton who at one time intended his son for the ministry of the Anglican church. But Fox grew up despising the clergy, whose religious and moral standards were not his. At 19 he left home, possessing, as he states in his journal, "wherewith both to keep myself from being chargeable to others, and to administer something to the necessities of others". For the next few years he was a wanderer, now in London, now back in Leicestershire, all the time in great mental turmoil. By the time he was 24 his great preaching mission had begun. His powerful voice, patent sincerity and commanding presence drew the crowds, and his powers of leadership and organising genius soon turned his followers into a formidable new religious sect. He preached of the light within each individual which came direct from God; he taught that there was no enlightenment to be had from intermediary clergy, who, in his eyes, got in the way.

It followed that baptism, marriage in church, eucharist or

burial in a churchyard must be firmly rejected, Tithes were withheld defiantly in the face of sometimes violent attempts by the local rector to secure them. The early minute-books reveal the strength of feeling about such matters and the care taken to ensure that members obeyed the rules.

ORGANISATION

The Society of Friends is above all else a religious body and the devotional life has always been paramount. From the beginning worshipping groups met two or three times weekly to "wait on the Lord", the silence broken only by spontaneous prayer or other ministry inspired by the holy spirit. Not surprisingly the refusal to attend the parish church (in itself a violation of the law), their obvious contempt for the incumbent and their refusal to pay tithe or church rate provoked hostility from the parish priest; and because they refused to swear oaths on the Bible in God's name and were consequently unable to swear an oath of allegiance to the Crown they found themselves, in the troublous days of mid-seventeenth century England, at odds with the civil authorities also. Persecution was severe.

It followed that for mutual protection it was necessary to organise what was, in effect, a self-supporting and self-regulating community. (The way in which this bound the Society into a cohesive and formidable social force will appear later). Members of the worshipping groups naturally concerned themselves with each others' protection and welfare. By 1667, such had been the growth of the movement, the establishment of agreed rules and procedures common to all could wait no longer.

Fox was a visionary. But he was also a brilliant organiser, and the foundations of church government which he laid remain to this day. His leadership did not go unopposed. Not surprisingly in that day and age his insistence that meetings for the conduct of church affairs must be open to all members as of right and that men and women must share responsibility equally provoked controversy which led to a short-lived but highly damaging "Separatist"[1] schism. But good sense prevailed in the main body of the church and men and women continued to share equally the joys and sorrows, the responsibilities and the prison sentences, the scourgings and the obscenities of stocks and pillory, the ministry and the caring.

MONTHLY AND QUARTERLY MEETINGS

Fox records in his journal that monthly meetings for the management of church affairs in Wiltshire were set up in 1668. The earliest minute-books we have are those for Chippenham Men's Monthly Meeting which date from 1669. No early minute-books of Women's Monthly Meetings are known to exist but meetings were indeed held, as we know from a minute of Wiltshire Quarterly Meeting of July 1698 which proposed that in future the men's and women's monthly meeting and half-yearly meetings might take place "at ye same time and place tho' distinct". The only minute-book of a Women's Monthly Meeting in Wiltshire which is known to exist is that for the years 1798 to 1818.

In Wiltshire in Fox's day there were Monthly Meetings centred on Charlcutt, Chippenham, Sarum, Lavington and Melksham. Each Monthly Meeting administered the worshipping groups (called Particular Meetings) in its locality; there were then some 23 of these in the county. No records of Melksham or Sarum Monthly Meetings are known to exist but happily we have some for Charlcutt, Chippenham and Lavington. From these early minute-books we know that matters brought before Monthly Meeting would include applications for permission to marry and arrangements for the solemnisation of marriage[2], support for members in prison or otherwise suffering at the hands of the authorities, the keeping of registers of births, marriages and deaths of members, support for widows and orphans, disownment (termination of membership), encouragement of marital fidelity, discouragement of sexual promiscuity and, in general, all matters relating to the maintenance of high standards of morality and integrity in a close-knit religious community. The early minute-books show that many procedures established in the seventeenth century continue to this day. We note, for example, that, although every member is entitled to attend meetings for church affairs, it is the custom to name one or two members from each Particular Meeting to do so, and these names are recorded in the minutes.

In the early days each county had its Quarterly Meeting. As with Monthly Meeting all members of the Society were encouraged to attend, and likewise Monthly Meetings and Particular Meetings were asked to appoint representatives and the names of these were included in the minutes. The earliest Quarterly Meeting whose minutes we have was held at Devizes on 1 April 1678. It is from these minute-books that we know that there was a Monthly Meeting for the Melksham area, though no other record of it has survived, and that there was a Monthly Meeting based on the Chippenham area from at least 1669, the earliest year for which we have minutes.

The Friends who met at Quarterly Meeting in April 1678 did so under great stress. There were only two items to consider and record in a new book. One was the routine appointment of two members to attend the next general meeting in London. The other recorded sadly "an occasion of disturbance" when "in a very unfriendly manner" some Separatists "katched up and carried away ye Quarterly Booke from ye Meeting ... and would not send it again or Returne themselves Although some Friend went to them from ye Meeting and Earnestly desired it of them". The Separatists also made off with the Quarterly Meeting funds and neither these, nor, alas, the pre-1678 minute-book were ever recovered.

From notes at the beginning of this new book, clearly intended as a reminder to members of their duties at this difficult time, we learn that Quarterly Meeting saw itself as responsible for policy and overall supervision of Monthly and Preparative Meetings (as Particular Meetings came to be called) throughout the county. It called for regular reports of anything of moment; it maintained a record of persecution ("sufferings") with full details of monetary losses and imprisonments; it kept a watch on gifts and bequests to ensure that money was properly spent where it was needed; it supervised the keeping by Monthly Meetings of births, marriages and burials; and it kept a sharp lookout for the wayward.

YEARLY MEETING
The annual gathering of all members, in the early days held sometimes in London, sometimes elsewhere (often Bristol) but nowadays called London Yearly Meeting and usually held in London. Yearly Meeting stands at the vertex of the organisational pyramid, makes policy and issues directives.

CLERKS, SCRIBES, CASHIERS AND REGISTRARS
Although the seventeenth century nomenclature is often different from that in use today duties and methods are remarkably similar. Then, as now, meetings for business were held in a spirit of worship. The clerk of the meeting is both chairman and secretary in one. The clerk's function is to discern the divine will as it may be revealed through the words of those present. The minute is roughed out and tried on the meeting; such amendments as are deemed necessary are made; and when the minute is finally approved it is left to be written up neatly in the minute-book.

In the early days this was the duty of the scribe who was also expected to make copies of important documents and perform such other similar duties as his skill and knowledge allowed. The minutes show that the scribe was paid for these tasks as they were performed.

The registrar recorded births, marriages, deaths and burials and instances of persecution. Like the scribe he was paid for what he did. The Wiltshire register of births and burials goes back to 1648, the marriage register to 1657; copies of these registers are in the Wiltshire County Record Office.

The cashier was, in today's terms, the treasurer.

ELDERS, OVERSEERS AND RECORDED MINISTERS[3]

Elders are the spiritual leaders, overseers concern themselves with the worldly needs of the membership, and recorded ministers are those deemed to be of sound sense and judgment who speak well. They are all specifically appointed by Monthly Meeting.

NOTES

1. The Separatists were led by John Wilkinson and John Story, both of Westmorland, who had been sent to Wiltshire as "publishers of truth" but came to reject George Fox's liberalism which allowed every member, regardless of sex or social standing, an equal voice in the running of the Society. They had substantial support in the county. *See also* page 121, note 1.

2. A marriage not in the parish church called for much more than registration, of course, and the rules were strict. Both parties must be members of the Society. They had to appear in person before both men's and women's Monthly Meetings. The Monthly Meeting would appoint two persons to look into the applicants' background and report back. If the marriage was approved a meeting for worship would be arranged at which all present would sign the marriage certificate. If the marriage was not approved and the couple married "by a priest", they ran grave risk of disownment by the Monthly

Meeting. If disowned they were no longer eligible to attend meetings for business, though they could still attend meetings for worship like any other member of the public.

Quaker marriages were accepted as valid in common law from 1661 when at Nottingham assizes an action which challenged the legitimacy of offspring thereof was lost. They did not, however, receive specific statutory recognition till 1753.

3. Although Friends shunned anything which suggested priesthood, articulate members who showed qualities of spiritual leadership were "recorded" or "acknowledged" by their Monthly Meeting. As in all branches of the Society's activities, women had equal status with men, and many of them were outstanding. Samuel Johnson's gibe comparing a Quaker woman minister preaching to a dog walking on its hind legs — "It is not done well; but you are surprised to find it done at all" was as inaccurate as it was insulting. Many women Friends "travelled in the ministry".

The practice of recording ministers was discontinued in 1924.

2   THE EARLY YEARS

There were Quakers in West Wiltshire from the late 1650s. They held their meetings in barns or in private homes and some-times, in spite of the dangers — for many years Quaker Meetings were unlawful — had their own meeting-house. They pos-sessed their own property at Corsham in 1659, probably the building at Monk's Lane now owned by the United Reformed Church. By 1660 they were meeting at Cumberwell (Fran-kleigh) just outside Bradford on Avon, probably already in property known to be owned by them in 1676, now a cottage[1]. At Slaughterford they met at first in a "great barn" in which in 1663 Fox preached[2]. By 1673 they owned property there — the ruins of a purpose-built meeting-house may still be seen[3]. There were meetings at Bromham, Calne, Chippenham, Devizes, Warminster, Lavington and other places.

Of these early Wiltshire Quaker centres, only at Melksham were Friends to maintain regular meetings for worship without a break from before 1669 up to the middle of the present century.

The Meeting at Shaw Hill

The genesis of Melksham Friends Meeting was the home of Robert and Hester Marshman at Shaw Hill, two miles out of the town itself. The Marshmans and their home first appear in the record when in 1669 some 80 Quakers are known to have met there, (probably for monthly Meeting)[4]. Before the Tolera-tion Act[5] removed the risks of such unlawful activities the Marshmans' home at Shaw Hill was far enough out of town not to attract unwelcome attention from the authorities.

Chippenham Monthly Meeting, of which Shaw Hill was a constituent, met there regularly and Robert and Hester's son Richard married Ann Rogers there in 1670.

Between 1678 and 1684 Shaw Hill Meeting embraced Corsham and Melksham, suggesting a single congregation meeting at more than one location as appropriate. After 1684 Corsham is listed separately and in 1690 their "house called the Meeting House" there was registered under the new legislation.

In 1690 the Marshman home was registered as a place of religious worship[6]; Robert having died in 1679 the registration was made in the name of his widow Hester (1600-1702). Registered at the same time was the house of Thomas Bevin (Beaven) who also belonged to Shaw Hill Meeting and regularly attended Quarterly Meeting as their representative between at least April 1689 and September 1695. After 1690 it was possible to meet anywhere without risk of disturbance and from then on, for most members, Melksham town will have been a more convenient rendezvous. From 1695 Shaw Hill Meeting no longer appears in the records, doubtless because its members were now meeting in Melksham itself.

Nevertheless the vicinity of Shaw and Shawhill continued as a Quaker stronghold, with Marshmans in the lead, into the early years of the eighteenth century. Robert and Hester's son Richard and their daughter Prosper were active Friends. By the time of his father's death in 1679 Richard had acquired the property at Shaw now called the Old Malthouse. His widow Ann and son Richard continued to live there after his death in 1694 and it is probably then that the adjoining burial ground (*see* next chapter) was inaugurated. Richard's son Richard died in 1709 and his son John in 1721.

Thomas Smith of neighbouring Shaw House wrote in his Diary[7] on Tuesday 28 February 1721:

> After dinner I was at the House late of John Marsh-
> man my Neighbour whose Corps was this Day to
> be put into the Earth in his own Orchard, the
> burying Place of his family, and several other
> Quakers. So after being in the Company of several
> of that Profession for about half an hour or more
> I return'd to my own Home when they carried the
> Corps into the Barn, where was to be a great
> Meeting a Cumberland [word omitted] being itiner-
> ante in the Parts and there to perform the Part of
> a Preacher.

It is clear from this that in 1721 a Marshman home was still very much a Quaker centre. Later on in the century the Marshman family, like so many other former Wiltshire Quaker families, turned elsewhere for their spiritual needs[8].

The Meeting in the town itself

The congregation which grew up in the town and a few years later acquired its own meeting-house in what is now King Street was probably strongest numerically between 1690 and 1730. Lists of members were not kept then but there are some 30 different family names in the records for those years and since the Society was very much a family matter this suggests a community of two or three times that number. Sufficient to themselves and largely avoiding social contact with what they called 'the world's people' they held no public office (as Dissenters they were debarred) and so took no direct part in town affairs. But as employers and wielders of economic power their influence was undoubtedly substantial.

Congregations then will have been large. Besides members of the Society there will have been those who, like Charles Lamb a century later, enjoyed the Quaker way of worship but did not wish to commit themselves to membership, with all its obligations. Small wonder that the vicar, Bohun Fox, was worried, as we shall see.

NOTES

1. O.S. map reference ST 821625 — near Pottick's House. Meeting outside a town afforded a measure of protection against molestation but did not always help. Bradford on Avon Quakers held their meetings at Frankleigh which they called Cumberwell. But in May 1660 they were set upon by a squad of troopers while at worship there. The soldiers carried off Robert Storr. Though charged with no offence Storr was imprisoned at Salisbury as one deemed "dangerous to the government". (Source: A Collection of the Sufferings of the People called Quakers, Chapter II page 39. Pub 1753).

2. The Journal of George Fox.

3. O.S. map reference ST 842738.

4. Victoria County History, volume 7, quoting G. Lyon Turner: *Original Records of early Non-conformity.*

5. More precisely: *An Act for Exempting their Majestyes Protestant Subjects dissenting from the Church of England from the penalties of certaine Laws. 1 Gul & Mar c¯18.* The Act came into force on 24 May 1689.
  The statute owed much to Quaker parliamentary lobbying and this is reflected in the text of it. Section X specifically absolved Quakers from the obligation to swear an oath when formally declaring allegiance to the Crown. Section XIII exempted them and other Protestant dissenters from the "laws for divine service". (Since the reign of Edward VI the law had required "diligent and faithful resort" to an Anglican place of worship. The penalty for non-attendance had been a fine of one shilling on each occasion, with prison for failure to pay.) To obtain the protection of the law their places of worship had to be registered with the authorities.
  Early Quakers were given to tackling "parliament men" as they called them. They even rented a coffee-house hard by the Houses of

Parliament to facilitate the practice. So effective were they that a contemporary writer, Francis Bugg, was moved to complain in a paper addressed to Parliament that what Parliament did one day was made null and void by the Quakers the next day.

6. WRO 854/14.

7. At page 154. (WRO161/170)

8. In her will made in 1810 Mary Marshman left £100 to Young Sturge and Cyrus Ovens "to be applied by them for the benefit of the Bath Monthly Meeting". Friends were uncertain about how she intended the money to be used and she was not, they noted, a member of the Society of Friends. (WRO1798/4 - Trusts and Trust Properties vested in Bristol and Somerset Quarterly Meeting of Friends page 40).

3 THE MEETING HOUSE AND THE BURIAL GROUNDS

By the late 1690s Melksham Quakers, who up to 1695 had based themselves on Shaw Hill, acquired a meeting place in what is now King Street. It came to them through the good offices of Simon Shewring (died 1721), of Canhold. The plot of land on which it stood had at one time belonged to William Rutty, yeoman, of Melksham, who left it to his son John (died 1696) cordwainer (shoemaker) of Melksham Meeting. When John died Simon Shewring proved the will as sole executor and in the course of winding up the estate sold to Melksham Friends for £10 "a piece and parcell of ground ... together with one messuage or tenement lately erected and built ..." (conveyance dated 20 December 1698)[1].

From this it seems likely that shortly before his death John Hancock had built a meeting-house for Friends' use on his land and that Simon Shewring, his executor, used his discretion to sell it to them for a sum low even by the prices of the day.

In about 1705 the building was extended; at Quarterly Meeting in May that year we find Melksham Friends being congratulated on their good work of "enlarging their meeting-house". This building sufficed till late 1776 or early 1777, when they built themselves a brand new one[2] on the same site. (The building is now owned by the National Spiritualist Church).

The cottages on either side of the meeting-house, numbers 10 and 16 King Street, were acquired later. (*See* Appendix G).

The burial ground behind the meeting-house was enlarged from time to time as the need arose. Since 1958 most of it has been cleared to make a garden and only the more recent gravestones now remain in place.

The meeting-house went out of use as such in 1950. In its day it had accommodated the longest-continuing Quaker congregation in Wiltshire. But that congregation had been dwindling since before the beginning of the century. After 1950 the meeting-room was rented to Plymouth Brethren and part of the rest of the building, which had earlier been used as the county library, became a library store. In 1958 it was sold, together with the adjoining cottages[3].

A burial ground at Shaw

Early Quakers cared little where their mortal remains were buried so long as it was not in a churchyard; the important thing was to have no truck with the Anglican church. Quaker burial grounds consequently evolved under pressure of events. When a death occurred something had to be done urgently, so a fellow Quaker would offer a space on his or her land. Other interments would follow. Usually, in due course, the plot would be marked off and ownership vested in the Society[4].

In a corner of a meadow adjoining the house known as The Old Malthouse at Shaw there are some half dozen horizontal gravestones bearing the following inscriptions:-

> Hester Marshman wife of Robert died September 1702 aged 102.

> Prosper Marshman died 9 May 1706.

> John Marshman died 2 March 1766 aged 52 and Betty Marshman widow of John died 15 February 1782 aged 63.

> Ann wife of John Pountney. Henry son of John.

Elizabeth daughter of Richard Marshman died April [day and year not distinguishable.]

Richard Marshman junior.

This is the burial-ground referred to in his diary by John Smith of Shaw House (*see* previous chapter). It was probably first used on the death of Richard in 1694. All those commemorated are members of the Marshman family.

The Quaker registers do not record any of these burials but they do record the following ones for which there are no gravestones:-

1702.9.26   At Shaw Rebecca Sartaine, widow.

1721.2.16   At Shaw Simon Shewring.

1743/4.1.13 At Shaw in the parish of Melksham, Joan[5] Pinnock, widow of Richard Pinnock senior.

1786.5.13   At James Marshman's burial ground at Shaw William Cookworthy of Melksham, surgeon, aged 35.

1807.8.16   At Mary Marshman's burying ground at Shaw Richard Rutty of Melksham aged 74.

Gravestones in an early Quaker burial-ground, above all ones inscribed with the names of months (February, March, April, September) which early Quakers refused to use, are anomalous. A directive of London Yearly Meeting in 1717 forbade gravestones and called for the removal of any already in place[6]; and as for the inscriptions, from the very beginning Quakers shunned what they called the pagan names for months (and days), using only the appropriate number, even in everyday speech.

We can deduce from this that the stones were installed, perhaps some years after the interment, by members of the Marshman family who had ceased to be Quakers, though some of those commemorated — Hester and her two daughters Prosper and Ann Pountney — certainly had been. Though The Old Malthouse remained Marshman family property until 1817 when Mary Marshman and her son James sold up[7]. family allegiance to the Society of Friends seems likely to have faltered, which is probably why the burial ground was never taken into formal ownership by the society. The Marshmans may have become Baptists; the name comes up again in the registration in May 1813 of a Baptist meeting-house at Shaw Hill "belonging to James Marshman"[8].

NOTES

1. Trusts and Trust Properties vested in Bristol and Somerset Quarterly Meeting and its Subordinate Meetings, page 78 (WRO 1798/4).

2. At the quarterly meeting held on 24 March 1777 those appointed to attend the yearly meeting in London were instructed to report "one new meeting-house built at Melksham"; a deed executed in the same year also describes the building as newly built.

3. At auction in 1958 the meeting-house, burial-ground and number 16 King Street were sold in one lot for £1300, and number 10 as a separate lot for £410. Both houses were tenanted, number 10 by Miss Park, who paid £10 a year for it and number 16 by Frank Brown Hiscock, who paid £24.14s.(WRO 1798/2). *See also* Appendix G.

4. Sometimes a meeting-house would, later on, be erected near by,

but often they remained separate, sometimes isolated. (*See* Appendix B).

5. Joan had married first Simon Shewring, who died in 1721. She re-married in 1722 Richard Pinnock of Inmarsh, Melksham, yeoman.

6. In 1850 policy was changed and Monthly Meeting was given discretion to authorise them subject to conditions. Where permitted, stones must be of uniform size, so as to guard against social distinction, and give name, age and date of death only.

Friends did not always comply strictly with the 1717 directive. Bartholomew Deeke's family, for example, decided that a tombstone would be desirable when they buried him in his garden at Seend Row. The stone, which bore the date 1738.6.1, was subsequently built into a cottage. (*Wiltshire Notes and Queries* 1908, Vol VI page 182).

7. For information about Marshmans at the Old Malthouse I am indebted to the report for the Wiltshire Buildings Record made by Barbara and Robert Harvey.

8. *Wiltshire Meeting House Certificates 1689-1852*: John Chandler, Wiltshire Record Society. Item 755 on page 73. Other registrations in the Melksham district involving Marshmans listed by Dr Chandler are: Joseph Marshman at Whitley in 1699 (item 77J); Zebulan ("Sibellan") Marshman in Melksham in 1714 (item 198) and again in 1716 (item 205) (Zebulan was pastor at the Baptist Church in Broughton Road). Another Marshman, James, was party to a Baptist registration in Trowbridge in 1812 (item 745), the premises registered being occupied by Robert Marshman.

4 SCHOOLS

As early as the 1660s national leaders of the movement had urged the setting up of schools for the children of members. By 1671 there were at least fifteen Quaker boarding-schools in England and a number of other establishments conducted by individual Friends. George Fox himself set up a school for boys and girls at Waltham Abbey and one for girls only at Shack-lewell (Hackney) "to instruct young lasses and maidens in whatsoever things are civil and useful in the creation".

Wiltshire Quakers had been talking about starting a school since at least 1691. A directive from Bristol Yearly Meeting in 1695 spurred them on:

> This meeting do desire that where Friends can they
> would get such schools and schoolmasters for their
> children as may bring them up in the fear of the
> Lord and love of his truth so that they may not only
> learn to be scholars but Christians also.

In Bristol itself there had been a Quaker school since at least 1668, when, for £10 a year, John Tappin was required to teach "so many of poor children as shall be thought convenient by this meeting". The meeting-house was used as the schoolroom. Later (1676), after the Friars meeting house had been erected, an empty room there was put to use.

In September 1696 a school was opened in Melksham under John Jefferys, from Hampton, Gloucestershire. Jefferys had been recommended to Wiltshire Friends by Nailsworth Meeting.

At first Friends were reluctant to use the new facility and

enquiries revealed that some had misgivings about the curriculum and the schoolmaster himself. Others stated that they could not afford the fees. A committee of three Melksham Friends, William Smith, Thomas Beaven and John Rutty and one Bradford one, John Clarke, was asked to look into the matter and report. As a result fees were adjusted according to ability to pay. In the course of discussion at Quarterly Meeting in April 1697 Jefferys was enjoined to "officiate his office as well by example as precept that they may be educated in truth as well as outward learning".

Things improved to Friends' satisfaction; the committee was able to report to the Quarterly Meeting in June that all was going well. They further reported that Simon Shewring had offered "to table children at a good table at £7 per annum, at a better for £9 per annum". This will have been for full board and lodging and was roughly comparable with what was charged at Friends' schools elsewhere[1].

Shewring (died 1721) was a man of substance, a recorded minister in Melksham Meeting and generally in very good standing among Friends. His offer to board children in his home will not have been motivated by a wish to profit but from a concern to enable children living at a distance to attend the school, which did not then take boarders.

Doubtless because of the boarding facility the school expanded and at Quarterly Meeting a year later (September 1698) we find Jefferys putting in for more commodious accommodation. At the quarterly meeting in April the following year a move to Devizes was proposed. The proposal was not, however, followed up.

Although Quakers, thanks to the Toleration Act, were now shielded from the worst excesses of persecution under the law, the statute was not a complete protection. In September 1702 Jefferys reported to Quarterly Meeting that two persons (unnamed) had consulted a lawyer "to prosecute him for keeping a school upon account of the Abjuration Act". Laws still in force could be invoked to preserve the Church of England monopoly in education, and in other parts of the country at least twelve Quaker schoolmasters were prosecuted between 1689 and 1718, when the law was finally reformed[2].

In the event no action was taken against Jefferys. Thomas Beaven (died 1735), well-known in the town as a successful clothier and sergemaker, a man of forceful personality and a formidable adversary had been instructed by Quarterly Meeting to speak to those who might be able to influence the troublemakers and this may well have done the trick.

Jefferys was not only "county schoolmaster" but, as a man of education, also scribe to Quarterly Meeting. This was paid work. The Quarterly Meeting minute-book records in July 1705, for example, that he was paid one guinea which included payment for "making the lease for Purton Meeting House".

Jefferys left Melksham in 1705 probably to live in London, where he was certainly living in 1734, and in good standing as we know from the fact that his name appears in a Quaker property deed of December that year.

His successor was John Padley, "a young man from the north". There were then 30 pupils. In February 1706 we find Quarterly Meeting welcoming a proposal by Padley to take boarders at the school. But by February the following year he has left, apparently abruptly, taking with him some Quarterly Meeting papers which do not seem to have been recovered; at Lavington Monthly Meeting in January 1709 "Melksham ffriends report from Abraham Mathews yt his certificate being given to Thomas Padly is at present lost". We find Adam Gouldney of Chippenham being asked to take over work on the "county register" which Padley has left unfinished.

The school seems to have continued, but under whose direction is not shown in any extant record. At Quarterly Meeting in January 1712 it is referred to as the "ffree school at Melksham for poor Friends Children"; Simon Shewring is asked for a copy of the will of John Hancock (died 1696) in the matter of the bequest to it of £10. The probability is that local Friends — perhaps Simon Shewring among them, given his known concern — decided to try to keep it going until a really satisfactory schoolmaster could be found. It does seem to have closed for a while, to re-open under Thomas Headley Bennet.

In Bennet Friends had found the man they were looking for. At first there seems to have been some uncertainty about premises and Devizes was suggested as a better location. But in the event they seem to have decided, for the time being at least, to keep the school at Melksham. In April 1722 Thomas Bennet reported to Quarterly Meeting that he intended to begin the following week; and Quarterly Meeting exhorted Friends in the county to "encourage him all yt they can and send as many Children to him as possible". But things did not go according to plan. By next Quarterly Meeting Bennet's father, John Litchfield Bennet, had died at his home in Jamaica and Thomas, his executor, had been given leave of absence to wind up the estate and was in Bristol, waiting for a ship. We hear no more of Bennet or the school until October 1724 when Chippenham Monthly Meeting agree his proposal to set up at Pickwick.

At Pickwick a year later there was a last attempt at per-secution. Samuel Twiford, who was in charge of the "free school" at Corsham[3], tried unsuccessfully to prosecute Bennet "for teaching a Grammar School". He was wasting his time and money as the law had changed some years before and education was no longer a Church of England monopoly.

We know a little more about the school and its staff after the move to Pickwick. We know, for example, that it was co-educational, but with boys and girls in separate class-rooms. And we pick up the names of some of the teaching staff. We learn of the name of an apprentice of Bennet's through the fact

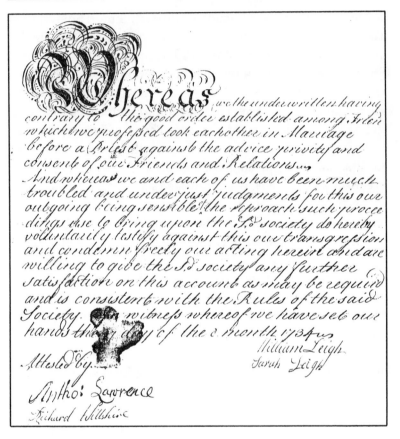

The Testimony of Repentance that William and Sarah Leigh were called upon to sign for having married 'before a priest'. Under the rules of the day they were also required to read it out at the close of Meeting for Worship. The practice was discontinued in 1801.

William was an apprentice at the Quaker School at Pickwick conducted by Thomas Headley Bennet.

that he has incurred the displeasure of Friends. In 1734 Chippenham Monthly Meeting records that William Leigh "hath clandestinely married Sarah, daughter of Anthony Lawrence of Brinkworth by a priest". Leigh was summoned to appear twice before Friends at monthly meeting and with Sarah to make a written admission of transgression before witnesses, of whom one was Sarah's father, the other Richard Wiltshire. Not long after we hear of Jonas Binns, presumably an assistant master, who has left and in respect of whom Friends find themselves unable to give a clear certificate of conduct.

A more satisfactory staff member was John Gough (1721/91) who came from Kendal and was appointed an assistant in 1735 at the age of fourteen. He stayed for four years then left for Ireland with a good recommendation from Monthly Meeting. He spent the next twenty years as a schoolmaster in Dublin, then in 1774 was appointed headmaster of the well-known Quaker school at Lisburn. His successor at Pickwick was Anthony Hatsell, also from Kendal.

Two pupils of the schools started by Melksham Quakers, first at Melksham, then at Pickwick, went on to achieve national distinction crowned by entries in the *Dictionary of National Biography*. One was Dr John Rutty (1698-1775). The other was Richard Reynolds (1735-1816), "father of the Industrial Revolution."

Reynolds, son of Bristol Quaker iron merchant Richard (died 1769) and Jane Dunn (or Doane), started school at Pickwick on 11 April 1741. He was five and a half years old. He rode the twenty-odd miles from Bristol on horseback accompanied only by a local carrier. As was usual in those days there were no regular school holidays but Richard Reynolds does seem to have made the occasional visit home to Bristol, to return with twopence pocket money.

School in the eighteenth century was rough and tough. Even the gentle Quakers used the birch on delinquents, though

Richard Reynolds (1735 - 1816), the renowned Quaker ironmaster, was educated at the Friends' School, in his day relocated at Pickwick but earlier (from 1696) located at Melksham.

evidently less freely than was customary elsewhere. Academic standards were high, likewise moral and religious ones. But the young Quakers, and Reynolds in particular, were not always as peaceable or well-behaved as their elders could have wished. We hear of an occasion when Reynolds formed a gang and set out to raid, on some pretext, the Church of England school[4]. They were, however, received so kindly by the Anglicans that their aggression evaporated and they came away friends[5].

Reynolds left school on 7 September 1750 aged nearly 15. As letters exchanged in later years with his old headmaster show, his time there seems to have been happy even though, on his own admission, his conduct was not always beyond reproach.

Headmaster Thomas Bennet's reputation among local Friends was high. He was active in Quaker affairs, regularly representing Melksham at Quarterly and Yearly Meetings. Monthly Meeting was frequently held in his home. He served as both clerk and scribe and was also a recorded minister. In 1724 he married Mary (died 1778) daughter of James Moggs, a Bristol cheesemonger.

After Bennet's death in September 1764 the school seems to have gone downhill. His son John took over[6] but by 1773 we find him described as a weaver. He died in 1802, described then as a yeoman. We do not again hear of a Friends school until about 1804 or 1805, when Edward Ash (1797-1873), who later became a medical practitioner, was sent to school at Melksham from Bristol at the age of seven or eight[7] and came under the influence of Rachel Fowler (1767-1833), wife of Robert (1755-1825). Robert was concerned for the education of children of the poor and planned to build a free school in Melksham, for which he bought a plot of ground. But his plans seem to have been thwarted.

The tradition of Quaker-run schools in Melksham lingered

well into the nineteenth century. There was a small boarding-school in Devizes Road run by Thomas Ferris. Ferris's son-in-law Henry Baron Smith, writing at the turn of the century[8] recalls that Ferris's daughter Maria had "a class for juniors" and that his pupils occupied several forms in the Friends Meeting House.

At some time between 1842 and 1856 Thomas Ferris gave up the school and become a grocer[9]. His house was taken over by Emma Sturge (born 1826) of Melksham Meeting. and, noted Smith, "very careful was the regime under which its inmates lived". In 1871 Emma, now a widow, was still running the school, which was known as The Lawn, (address The Spa). She was assisted by her three unmarried daughters Ellen (born 1845), Hannah (born 1846) and Rebecca (born 1850). There were ten pupils, aged between eight and eighteen.[10] In 1881 Emma Sturge was still in business. Hannah was still teaching there but Ellen and Rebecca were not listed. Instead there was Lucy Ann Godson aged 23. There are three boarding pupils, Juliette Henry, aged 15, Amy Amelia Evans, aged 11 and Marie A Cotterell, aged 11[11]. Kelly's Directory shows that this establishment was still functioning in 1885, but by the turn of the century it was no longer listed. Times had changed.

NOTES

1. Around the same time, at Sidcot (Quaker) School in neighbouring Somerset, the inclusive fee of £9 was considered expensive. At Ackworth in Yorkshire some 80 years later fees were eight guineas (£8.8s) a year for education, board and clothing.

2. See W.C.Braithwaite: *The Second Period of Quakerism* (1921) pp 532/3.

3. Presumably the "free schoole and Almeshouse" near Corsham

Court which Dame Margaret Hungerford had founded in 1668.

4. This was probably the Dame Margaret Hungerford school.

5. As told by Reynolds's granddaughter Hannah Mary Rathbone in *A Memoir of Richard Reynolds* (1852).

On leaving school Reynolds returned to Bristol to serve a seven-year apprenticeship with Quaker grocer William Fry. Towards the end of the apprenticeship Thomas Goldney of Clifton, who was a partner of Abraham Darby in the running of the iron works at Coalbrookdale, engaged him to transact some business there. He met Darby's daughter Hannah and married her the following year. Shortly afterwards Abraham Darby died and Reynolds assumed charge of the extensive works at Coalbrookdale, then the most important ironworks in England. He was immensely successful. In 1789 he retired from business, determined, as he said, to accumulate no more wealth but to spend or give away his income year by year. In 1804 he retired to Bristol, home of his childhood, where he died at the age of 81.

6. Minute 6 of Wiltshire Quarterly Meeting held on 24 September 1764.

7. *Journal of the Friends Historical Society Vol X* and *Friends Annual Monitor* for 1875.

8. In handwritten "Melksham Memories 1870-1892" (unpublished) WRO 2269/33. See Appendix E.

9. The Quaker marriage register in the Wiltshire Record Office records this as his occupation when, in July 1856, his daughter Eliza, a teacher at the Quaker school at Sidcot, Somerset, married Henry Baron Smith a teacher at Weston-super-Mare.

Eliza had earlier been a governess in the family of Quaker William Simpson (born 1795, brushmaker, listed in Kelly's Directory for 1855 under Gentry) teaching daughters Mary (born 1832) and Elizabeth (born 1840). The Simpsons lived in Watson's Yard (also known as Watson's Barton) in the house now known as Leaze Cottage, 19 Watson's Court.

When Henry Baron Smith was courting Eliza he would, after a week-end in Melksham, catch the train on Monday morning and be in good time to give his first lesson at Weston super Mare.

10. 1871 Census.

11. 1881 census. See also Appendix E. An undated marginal gloss in different handwriting in Henry Baron Smith's *Memories* notes that "this house has now been razed to the ground and a more imposing one is built in its place".

5 TITHE TESTIMONY

We've cheated the parson, we'll cheat him again,
For why should the blockhead have one in ten?

Old song

Until their virtual abolition in the late nineteenth century tithe and church-rate were a constant source of friction. This form of tax on property for the maintenance of the parish church and the incumbent was widely resented. By George Fox's day it was a major political issue. Cromwell and his parliament fully intended to abolish it but neither lived long enough to do so.

The law remained in force. English non-conformists grumbled but continued to pay up and Irish Catholics reacted with bloody insurrection. The Quakers responded in their own way: they quietly decided that they could not accept that one religious body, whose doctrines and ritual they disapproved of, should thus impose their will upon another, and resolved that all Quakers must peaceably refuse payment. No rule of the Society of Friends was more rigorously enjoined. It was the London Yearly Meeting directive of 1706 and the penalties it recommended which so incensed Thomas Beaven II and gave rise to his angry letter of resignation that year (*see* chapter 8ii). It should be added that not every Friend was a scrupulous non-payer. But the policy propounded by the central body was uncompromising.

London Yearly Meeting not only forbade payment of tithe but also insisted that Friends should not be receivers as impropriators.[1] Many Friends doubtless saw lay impropriation as venial and in this connexion it is worth noting that John

Rutty, who was a resolute non-payer of tithe to vicar Bohun Fox, tolerated distraint by Henry Rutty and his wife Mary, non-Quakers, who, as reported by Rutty to Monthly Meeting in August and September 1704, took peas and barley 'not exceeding demand'. Perhaps Henry was a kinsman.

Apart from John Rutty, who suffered imprisonment, the testimony does not seem to have imcommoded Melksham Friends unduly. This may have been because most of them were secretly paying up. Indeed, in 1752, London Yearly Meeting singled out Wiltshire members (of whom Melksham Friends were a substantial component) for particular mention with the observation: 'There are some who pretend that they are not convinced that they ought not to pay them.'

In the neighbouring counties, by contrast, Friends experienced serious abuse. Gloucestershire, for example, was notorious for ill-treating Quaker tithe-refusers. In 1716 Jonathan Peasley of Olveston Meeting was committed to Gloucester prison, then to The Fleet, for unpaid tithe of £7. Everything he owed was seized and sold for £237. At Stroud as late as the 1820s a petition to the House of Commons protested about distraint of £438.15s. for a tithe of £270.11.11d. Hampshire was even harsher. In 1758 Daniel Hollis, after a lifetime of vicious persecution by the local vicar, John Gilbert, was, at the age of 97, assaulted and thrown into gaol, where he died a few days later.

For the local or family historian, at least, a happy consequence of the careful keeping of records of Quaker sufferings from the middle of the nineteenth century on is what they tell us of occupations and status beyond what may be gleaned from registers. In Wiltshire these run from 1653 to 1865[2].

NOTES

1. An impropriator was a lay owner of the right to collect tithe. Impropriation (Latin *in proprietatem*) was one of the fruits of the Reformation. When a monastery was dissolved the right to collect tithe passed, with its other property, to lay hands.

In law, tithe was the equivalent of an estate in land which could, like an advowson, be inherited, or bought and sold as an inverstment, like any other real property.

Impropriate tithe could also be created by a local parson, needing capital, assigning all or part of his entitlement to tithe in return for a lump sum.

It is not surprising that London Yearly Meeting should be down on Quaker owners for claiming tithes where other Quakers were being harassed, treated roughly and sometimes imprisoned for withholding them. Where there was firm evidence of tithe payment, disownment (expulsion) followed. Even suspicion could give rise to penalties. In 1697, for example, Israel Noyes of Calne, later of Bradford (died 1708) was stripped of his status and office of recorded minister because he would neither admit nor deny that he had paid.

2. There are four registers of sufferings in Wiltshire County Record Office: WRO 1699/17 and 18; WRO 854/50 and 51.

6 THE QUAKERS, THE VICAR, AND A WELL-DISPOSED JUSTICE OF THE PEACE

The Reverend Bohun Fox was vicar of Melksham from 1697 to his death in 1750. A newcomer to the district, just down from Oxford with a degree in law, he must have been dismayed to find in Melksham so much dissent.

The Baptists were bad enough. Fox wryly offered to baptize Zebulan Marshman, pastor of the Baptist church in Broughton Road, by total immersion if that was all he wanted. But at least Baptists paid their tithes and church-rate. Much more to be feared and resented was the then large and influential Quaker community whose objections to paying these dues threatened his very livelihood. So it is not surprising that he should pursue vigorously his rights to his emoluments.

Not all Melksham Quakers scrupulously refused payment. The records suggest that some of them, unable to take the tithe testimony seriously as an article of faith (and probably also reluctant to antagonise the vicar and his friends with whom, as tradesmen, many will have been doing business) were quietly paying up.

But there were also those who stuck by the rules and suffered accordingly. Prominent among them were John Somner, clothier, of Seend Row (fl. 1703), William Smith, clothier and maltster of Whitley (fl. 1705) and John Rutty (1671-1726), clothier, maltster, farmer, cheesemonger and keeper of shops (see later) all of them rich and influential, all of them vigorously prosecuted by Fox as tithe-refusers. John Rutty served two terms in Fisherton gaol in consequence. On one of the occasions it was for refusing an order to pay two years' tithe amounting to £41.12s and costs of £137, very substantial sums in those days; Rutty was clearly well-to-do.

Whatever Bohun Fox's views of Rutty's religious persuasion and intransigence he seems to have found it necessary to make purchases from his firm, John Rutty and Co. Given Rutty's uncomprising attitude one can picture his annoyance, recorded by Monthly Meeting in March 1714, at finding that his partners, without consulting him, have allowed Fox to set off a debt he owed the firm against tithes due to him from Rutty!

Other Melksham Quakers were clearly on excellent terms with the vicar and worked with him amicably in civic duties. When Isaac Selfe JP of Melksham, linsey-maker, landowner and leading local magnate, made his will in March 1740 he appointed his "well-beloved friends" Master Bohun Fox, Thomas Fuge, parish clerk, John Newman, clothier and George Brinkworth, maltster, to be his executors and the document was witnessed by Amos Sumption, Alce Andrews and Sam Rutty. Newman, Sumption and Rutty are readily identified as leading local Quakers. When Newman, jointly with Fox, obtained probate, it was officially recorded that being a Quaker, he affirmed[1]. Amos Sumption was John Newman's brother-in-law. Sam Rutty was clerk of Monthly Meeting.

To Isaac Selfe JP Bohun Fox dedicated his "Agrippa" pamphlet in the controversy with Thomas Beaven described in chapter 8. This particular Isaac Selfe does not seem to have been a member of the Society of Friends though the choice of a Quaker executor and two Quaker witnesses to his will suggests a fairly close connexion, as does the fact that others of the same family name had been Quakers from the movement's very beginning. In 1660 Isaac Selfe, of Market Lavington, had been sent to prison for non-payment of £40 tithe and remained there six years. This Isaac Selfe was again in trouble in 1670 when he was fined heavily on two occasions for allowing his house to be used for Quaker meetings; his son Isaac was fined for being present at one of them. In 1672 Isaac Selfe and Jane Selfe were both in the county gaol and in 1684 Mary Selfe of Bromham and others were arrested while at worship and imprisoned for five weeks[2]. It was Isaac Selfe's house at Market Lavington that was registered in 1690 under the Toleration Act as a Quaker place of worship.

But Isaac Selfe, the Melksham magistrate, though possibly kin, clearly held no such strong sectarian views. Public-spirited and on good terms with parson and Quaker alike he was evidently the sort of person to call upon for support where needed, whether the call came from vicarage or meeting-house. And so we find that it was to him that Friends of Lavington Monthly Meeting turned in January 1712 for support in the nation-wide Quaker campaign for a change in the law to allow for affirmation instead of the oath on all occasions, asking him to use his influence to this end with the local member of parliament, Colonel Lambert.

NOTES

1. Quakers refused, on religious grounds, to swear an oath. Before 1689 the authorities would tender the Oath of Allegiance to a member of the Society of Friends so as to have an excuse to send him or her to prison. The Toleration Act of 1689 put an end to this abuse by permitting Quakers to "affirm" their loyalty. As time went on, affirmation came to be accepted by the authorities wherever an oath was called for.

2. Joseph Besse: *A Collection of the Sufferings of the People called Quakers*, Volume II, Chapter 2, Wiltshire, page 39. (1753)

7 POOR FRIENDS

It was a firm rule that "necessitous" Friends must be helped out. Most Melksham Quakers were prosperous, but poor members did exist, and like Quaker Meetings elsewhere Melksham Friends tried to make sure that lack of means did not prevent such from playing a full part in the Society's activities. Help would also be forthcoming for members faced with temporary adversity or unforeseen emergency or needing help with schooling and apprenticeships.

In 1717 John Clarke and James Willett, both of Bradford on Avon, were asked to look into the matter of poverty at Melksham and to report back to Monthly Meeting, noting whether applicants were also receiving parish relief. We know little of the criteria for giving help but we may be sure that the case had to be a deserving one. The sick, the elderly, widows with young children and poor prospects of re-marriage, and elderly spinsters will have qualified.

Trust funds would often be set aside for such purposes[1]. We find that in 1770 Melksham Quaker clothier Dennis Newman left by will £50, the income from which was to be used for the relief of "second poor members of the Society of Quakers belonging to the Meeting of Melksham"[2].

In 1819 Robert Fowler, William Matravers and Mary Jefferys set up a trust which, though a first charge on the income from it was to be repairs and maintenance of Melksham meeting-house, what was left over was to be used to help Melksham Friends with education, apprentice fees, marriage portions and the expense of travelling to attend distant meetings.

Two case-histories can be pieced together from the records

by way of illustration. At Lavington Monthly Meeting in October 1716 a collection was taken for "Widow Wyly". This Friend was Hannah, daughter of William Butler, yeoman, of Sheldon, Chippenham. She had married Thomas Wyly, maltster, son of Jane Wyly, widow of Coleraine, Ulster, in 1702. When Thomas died Hannah was left with three children, Martha, aged 11, William nearly 9 and Hannah 7. Thomas had been in good standing among Friends and had represented Melksham Meeting at levels up to Quarterly Meeting. With no help to be had from Thomas's side of the family in Ireland and probably little if any from Hannah's, Friends stepped in. Little William was despatched to Bath and bound apprentice to Jacob Wakcome, whip-maker, Quarterly Meeting paying the apprenticeship premium of £5. Hannah did not re-marry and left Melksham, presumably to live with relatives. She died in 1750.

The plight of James Paine, broadweaver, was on the agenda of Lavington Monthly Meeting in June 1727. Paine had been ill for some time and unable to follow his trade. The rent of his cottage had been unpaid for the past three quarters and his landlady was dunning him with threats of distraint and eviction. He had joined the Society of Friends at Bradford on Avon and had been a member there for eight years. He had transferred to Melksham Meeting on his marriage in 1725 to a Melksham Friend, Mary, daughter of Francis Charles, a Melksham broadweaver. It was decided that the burden of relieving him should be shared equally between Melksham and Bradford on Avon Friends.

NOTES

1.*Trusts and Trust Properties vested in Bristol and Somerset Quarterly Meeting.* (WRO 1798/4)

2. In terms of parish relief the expression "second poor" was used to describe those who had fallen on hard times and needed a helping hand to tide them over. Those whose poverty was permanent, say through age, chronic sickness, accident or disability were designated "first poor".

8   WEIGHTY FRIENDS

(i) A miscellany of worthies

In December 1744 Wiltshire Quarterly Meeting decided that debts which had been mounting up over the past twenty years, partly as a result of lawsuits defending the legality of Quaker marriages, must be paid off. A fund-raising exercise was initiated[1].

Melksham Friends responded well. All nineteen members approached gave something and the total came to £16.10s. Only Corsham Meeting did better, eighteen out of nineteen approached donating a total of £22.7s. Melksham donors were as follows:

James Moore gave two and a half guineas[2], one of the two largest donations. He was the son of John, of Sarum. He married in 1733 Rachel Beaven, widow of Jeremiah Beaven who had died in 1730. A faithful attender at business meetings, he was regularly called upon to perform duties on behalf of Monthly and Quarterly Meeetings.

Thomas Beaven, Senior, (born 1698) (see later) gave two guineas.

Samuel Rutty (1695-1762) (see later) gave two guineas.

Samuel Sanger (1710-1787) gave two and a half guineas. He was the son of Henry, Warminster wool-stapler. Like his father. Samuel was a prosperous clothier and, apparently, from the fact that in 1751 he was using a malthouse and brewhouse at Melksham called The Ark[3], a maltster as well.

The Newman family gave generously. Paul Newman, Senior (1693-1760) gave one and a half guineas. He was the son of Paul, Melksham tailor (died before 1738) and Mary (died 1738). His wife was Elizabeth, born Lutley (died1749). It was Dennis who gave £50 in his will for "second poor Friends" (*see* note 2 to chapter 7).

Sons John (born 1729), Dennis (1720-1750) and Paul Newman, Junior (born 1722) gave respectively 7s.6d., 5s.6d and 5s.6d. All were clothiers.

Amos Sumption (died 1765) gave half a guinea. Amos was a joiner, son of William of Wraxall (died 1720). Paul Newman was his father-in-law and the young Newmans were his brothers-in-law, he having married in 1724 Paul's daughter Deborah. As noted elsewhere he was a witness to the will of Isaac Selfe JP.

John Reeves gave half a guinea. He was a husbandman at Bromham, son of William of Blackland, Calne. He married in 1712 at Melksham Elizabeth Robbins of Bradford on Avon, daughter of Matthew and Elizabeth, late of Calne. He sometimes represented Melksham Friends at Monthly Meetings.

Richard Stokes gave half a guinea. Of him I have found in the records nothing more.

Thomas Hunt gave half a guinea. He lived at Chalfield and Monthly Meeting met at his house there in February 1728. In 1728 and 1729 he represented Melksham Friends at Quarterly Meeting. Perhaps Elizabeth Hunt, who died at nearby Holt in 1789 aged 100 was his wife. On Jacob Hunt, who gave half a crown (2s.6d), the records are otherwise silent.

Thomas Beaven, Junior, gave half a guinea. He was the son of Thomas Beaven, Senior, and like him a clothier.

Jonathan Rutty (1723-1770) gave half a guinea. He was son of Samuel (1695-1762).

John Moxham (1722-1787) gave half a guinea. He married Esther, born Rutter (1730-1798). Esther was a recorded minister[4].

The Widow Marshman, who gave 5s. was probably Mary, born Berry, of Shaw, widow of Richard whom she had married in 1724. As we have seen, the Marshman family at Shaw and Shaw Hill were leading Melksham Friends from very early on.

Ann Harris gave 5s. The name does not seem to be on record anywhere else.

The Widow Jeffry who gave 5s. may have been Jane, married to David who died in 1739. Jane later moved to Calne and died there in 1751.

Other leading friends of Melksham Meeting or closely connected with it include:

John Clarke (died 1726). Clarke belonged to Bradford on Avon Meeting. He grew up in London, where he married in 1684 Ann Truss, daughter of widow Ann Truss of Reading Friends Meeting. He was then a cabinet-maker. He first appears in Wiltshire Quaker records in 1692, where he is described as "chemist and practitioner of physick", a rather startling instance of professional mobility in the early eighteenth century. He became clerk of Lavington Monthly Meeting and was clearly a very energetic one. His son John followed him in the practice of medicine.

John Hancock (died 1696), cordwainer (shoemaker). He was sent to prison for eleven months in January 1689 for withholding tithe. In his will he left £10 towards the cost of sending the children of poor Friends to the school at Melksham. His father Nathaniel had owned the one-acre plot and tenement which later became the meeting-house and burial-ground in King Street.

Samuel Hipsley (1748-1789) was a Melksham baker. His wife was Lydia (1747-1809). Their son Samuel (1773-1829) was also a baker in Melksham. The family are likely to have been of modest means and the name does not appear in the "sufferings" register until 1813 when we find household furniture to the value of £1.10s. taken from Maria Hipsley. In 1816 a table and chair worth 10s. were taken from her for unpaid church-rate of 2s. Another member of the Hipsley family, John (1741-1816), eldest son of Richard and Ann of Churchill, Somerset, married, in 1762, Elizabeth (1736-1811) daughter of John Selfe of Devizes. He set up as a baker in Bristol but later became headmaster of the Quaker school at Ackworth, where he earned a reputation for sternness.

Simon Shewring (died 1721) was at various stages in his life yeoman, tailor and surgeon. He was active in Lavington Monthly Meeting and was a recorded minister. He lived at Bradford on Avon until 1683, when he moved to Shawhill. In 1697 he moved to Melksham, lived there for the rest of his life and was buried at Shaw on 19 April 1721. He it was who, as executor of John Hancock's will, sold to Friends the land for the meeting-house and burial-ground. He took an active interest in the school at Melksham. His son Stephen became a tailor in Bradford on Avon.

NOTES

!. WRO 1699/115. The carefully drawn-up subscription list, clearly the work of scribe and schoolmaster John Bennet, reflects the diminishing strength of the Society in Wiltshire. The list contains 136 names in all, forty one in Lavington Monthly Meeting, fifty six in Chippenham Monthly Meeting and thirty nine in Charlcutt Monthly Meeting. The names will have been selected from among full members of the Society from whom a contribution was expected. By this time adult membership in the Quarterly Meeting was about 200.

The result of the appeal suggests a failure of support which would have been unthinkable half a century before. Of the sixteen Particular Meetings approached, seven gave nothing: these were Sarum (five names), Brinkworth (three names), Charlcutt (ten names), Purton (three names),Marlborough (four names), Devizes (five names) and Bromham (six names). Despite reminders the sum raised fell far short of the £162 needed and in April 1746 Quarterly Meeting decided to declare the appeal closed.

2. £2.12s.6d.

3. Kenneth Rogers: *Wiltshire and Somerset Woollen Mills* (1976), page 94.

4. The Moxhams had a son John, a bellows-maker, who, according to the Dictionary of Quaker Biography maintained at Friends House, London, (unpublished). quoting the *Annual Monitor*, "might be justly called the poor man's friend and counsellor and was esteemed by all classes". He was a recorded minister. He died in 1824 aged 72.

(ii) THE BEAVENS

There were Beavens in Melksham Meeting from early on in the Society's history. The name of Thomas Beaven, yeoman, appears in the minute-book of Chippenham Monthly Meeting when his daughter Millicent married Thomas Bayly of Pickwick in 1701. It is likely that it was this Thomas Beaven whose house, with Hester Marshman's, was registered in 1690 as a Quaker place of worship under the Toleration Act.

In April 1689 the name of Thomas Beaven appears in the minute-book of Wiltshire Quarterly Meeting (the earliest one extant) as representative for Shaw Hill Meeting, and continues to appear regularly over the course of the next few years. It seems likely that this Thomas Beaven, continuously active in Quaker affairs throughout his life but at the date of the registration as yet unmarried, and possibly living in the parental home, was the son and not the father.

This Thomas Beaven (hereafter "Thomas II") married Mary Hayward of Market Lavington in 1691 and died in 1735. Thomas II and Mary had a son Thomas ("Thomas III") born 1698. Thomas III married Elizabeth Sanger (died 1750) in August 1718. A son ("Thomas IV") was born on 7 August 1720.

Thomas II and Thomas III, both clothiers of standing, played a leading part in Quaker affairs. But both of them, in their respective ways, were destined to be, as related below, a source of embarrassment to Melksham Friends.

Two other members of the Beaven family, Roger and Jeremiah, were also prominent West Wiltshire Quakers. Roger, a maltster, was originally of Calne Meeting. From about 1712 he was at Melksham, by 1722 at Devizes[1], where Lavington Monthly Meeting, of which from February 1712 he was clerk, met regularly. Roger stoutly maintained the Quaker testimony against payment of tithe or church rate[2], He was a faithful attender at sessions of Quarterly Meeting, which in 1719 made him a trustee of the newly-erected meeting-house at Bradford on Avon. He regularly attended Yearly Meeting.

Jeremiah Beaven, contemporary with Roger, was a member of Melksham Meeting in good standing. We note that, for example, in 1726 Quarterly Meeting appointed him to attend London Yearly Meeting and that from time to time he performed trusteeship duties on their behalf.

The members of the Beaven family that we know most about are Thomas II and Thomas III.

Thomas Beaven II (died 1735)

Thomas II was a prosperous, energetic, formidable and sometimes cantankerous member. That his fellow Quakers put up with him is a tribute to their tolerance and to his capabilities and value to the movement. Throughout his life he served the Society well, being at various times Quarterly Meeting treasurer, auditor, clerk of Monthly Meeting and clerk of London Yearly Meeting.

Thomas II was a prolific author of tracts and pamphlets on Quaker religious principles. Most or possibly all of these were printed and circulated at his own expense. But at least one, *An Essay concerning the Restoration of Primitive Christianity in a Conduct truly pious and religious* was of sufficient merit to be reprinted twice, once with additions, evidently during his lifetime, and once again in 1793, long after his death in 1735[3].

The earliest of Beaven's pamphlets (19 September 1696) still extant is the follow-up to a debate between John Plympton, a Baptist, and John Clarke of Bradford on Avon which took place in the courtyard of Beaven's house at which William Penn was present and in which Plympton was bested[4].

He called this *John Plimpton: Ten charges against the People called Quakers briefly Answered.* He prepared it in association with Paul Knight, Simon Shewring and John Rutty and had it distributed at a meeting which Plympton, keen on a return bout, had announced for 22 September. (Neither Clarke nor

Beaven could attend Plympton's meeting as Quarterly Meeting at Chippenham had been fixed for that day and they clearly thought that more important,)

Other early printed matter originated by Beaven, copies of which are extant, include, in 1706/7, a battle of words with his own Monthly Meeting leading to one with the vicar, Bohun Fox. The one with Fox landed him briefly in gaol.

The year 1706 found Beaven at odds with members of Lavington Monthly Meeting, of which he was clerk, to an extent which precipitated his dismissal from that office and replacement by John Clarke, the Bradford on Avon medical practitioner.

It appears that Beaven felt outraged by a directive from London Yearly Meeting that year requesting that those known to be paying tithes, or, as impropriate tithe owners, receiving them, be excluded from Quaker business meetings.

His removal as clerk of Monthly Meeting in August and the decision of Quarterly Meeting the following month to implement the Yearly Meeting directive in spite of his strong opposition, sparked an explosion of resentment which found expression in a most offensive letter of resignation from the Society dated 12 October 1706 in which he accuses Friends of ganging up against him over many years with "injustice, hate and revenge". He singles out for particular castigation Henry Sanger (Warminster wool-stapler whose daughter Elizabeth was in 1718 to marry his son Thomas III) whom he describes as "ungrateful" and John Hodges (Warminster maltster) as "your conceited Oracle". In his description of the highly respected medical practitioner John Clarke, who had replaced him as clerk of Monthly Meeting, he descends to sneering abuse:

> Your effeminate Doctor (for so I call him,
> because he is a Midwife in Ordinary, to
> your shame, as well as his) ...

There follows a detailed criticism of Quaker customs and observances. Above all why should members be forced to withhold payment of tithe and church-rate on pain of expulsion? What was the purpose of refusing the sacraments of eucharist and baptism? Why reject hat honour[5] and insist on distinctive dress and language,[6] all based on nothing better than levelling principles? Why not have a chairman at meetings as other bodies did and put an end to the abuse of 20 or 30 speaking at once, the loudest voice prevailing? And why tolerate "poor ignorant brainsick fellows and Petty-coat Fathers[7] that love to fare well and live easy and have got assurance enough to undertake to speak in the name of the Lord with senceless and ridiculous Preachments..."?

Beaven had the effusion printed, evidently for distribution among Meeting members. One copy came before Lavington Monthly Meeting in November 1706 to be greeted, not surprisingly, with dismay. The vicar, Bohun Fox, got hold of a copy — his glee can be imagined — and had further copies made, presumably for general distribution in the town and among his congregation.

Monthly Meeting's immediate response to Beaven's outburst was to appoint a committee of eight, which included Clarke, Hodges and Sanger, to "give him a Visit and tenderly lay his outgoings before him, and desire him publickly to retract itt with all possible speed". This remarkable forbearance brought about a complete reconciliation. In February 1706/7 Lavington Monthly Meeting recorded that Beaven had "published a Retraction"" and requested the views of each Particular Meeting on it.

Beaven called his retraction *Second Thoughts in relation to the Quakers*. Bohun Fox made swift reply. By 20 February he had drafted comments on the retraction and had them printed in London together with copies of Beaven's original outburst and his retraction all bound together in the form of a booklet which he called *Agrippa*[8] *almost persuaded to be a Christian, or the Self-condemn'd Quaker,* He dedicated it to Isaac Selfe of Beanacre, Justice of the Peace.

Beaven riposted with a paper which he called *The High Priest of Melksham, his Reasonings, his Concessions and his Self-contradictions.* Describing himself with mock humility as a simple drugget-maker ill-equipped to parry the thrusts of so highly educated a man as the vicar he answered Fox's paper effectively enough. Unfortunately for himself he overdid things by repeating a story that Bohun Fox had bought his way into the Melksham living. For this the vicar had him arrested and held on a charge of criminal libel, "wilfully publishing a thing not true against his neighbour Parson Fox in the last page of his work The High Priest as if he gave guineas to come into his place at Melksham".

The vicar seems to have been determined to teach Beaven a lesson and at first refused to withdraw the prosecution, notwithstanding an attempt at mediation by Beaven's father. But Beaven does not seem to have been brought to trial.

At Monthly Meeting on 20 September 1708 he mentioned a further paper he was preparing by way of justification of his allegations against Bohun Fox. Not surprisingly Friends were alarmed and requested him to submit his effort to John Clarke, John Hodges and Jonathan Tyler, who were asked to supervise and correct as necessary. At the next meeting Clarke and Hodges reported that the paper was acceptable. But Friends were still apprehensive, and requested Beaven to submit first to them anything he might in future plan to publish.

Beaven went into print under the title *Some Observations on the Controversie lately depending between Bohun Fox, Vicar of Melksham and Thomas Beaven, Junr.* The paper is moderate in tone and doubtless reflects the supervision of the Friends appointed to edit it. In it he retracts the libel which, he states, was based on what Henry Rutty, the vicar's agent, had told him, whose words, Simon Shewring, being present, could confirm[9].

The episode is remarkable for the loving forbearance of Melksham Friends despite Beaven's tantrums, his rudeness to them, his gross exaggerations and the damage he had undoubtedly done to their reputation in the town. Gentle remonstrance seems to have won him over completely. In due course he became Quarterly Meeting treasurer, playing his part in Meeting affairs with sweet reasonableness. In the years 1716, 1719, 1723, and 1727 Friends at national level so far expressed their confidence in him as to entrust him with the clerkship of London Yearly Meeting.

In August 1722 we find him at Cullompton, with a group of other Friends, now himself "travelling in the ministry", (he was now a recorded minister) keen as ever on writing and proselytizing in support of Friends' tenets[10].

He died at Bristol in 1735.

Thomas Beaven III

Thomas III followed his father in the family clothing business as well as in the tradition of service to the Society of Friends. The picture of him that emerges from the records is of an energetic, highly reputable and much respected and trusted Friend. On 6 July 1718 Quarterly Meeting appointed him and Roger Beaven, and eight others, trustees of the new meeting-house at Bradford on Avon. In December 1718 he became Quarterly Meeting registrar. In July 1721 we find him and his father and Roger Beaven appointed to represent Quarterly Meeting at Yearly Meeting to be held at Taunton. Later on he became clerk of Lavington Monthly Meeting. On 10 February 1718 and again on 20 November 1722 (now married to Elizabeth Sanger) we find him acting as host to the peripatetic Thomas Story. (His father, Thomas II, was then back in Melksham, evidently living with his son and new daughter-in-law.) In Ben Street's will of 1730 we find Thomas III named as a trustee. When, in 1744, Wiltshire Quarterly Meeting sought to raise funds to defray certain debts[11], Thomas, with a donation of two guineas, was among the most generous; a more typical contribution by others was half a guinea and many who were asked gave nothing at all. But after 1747 Thomas's name no longer appears in Wiltshire Quaker records.

From other sources we learn that in 1748 he became bankrupt[12]. Contemporary press cuttings in the library of Wiltshire Archaeological and Natural History Society in Devizes[13] tell us what we fail to learn from the Quaker records.

It appears that when Thomas III's business failed he was harassed by his creditors to a degree which amounted to persecution. Although he made full disclosure of his assets they persistently refused to come to an arrangement which would permit his discharge from bankruptcy. Clearly at his wits' end to know what to do next while still striving to persuade his creditors to let him off the hook, he stumbled on what looked like a way out.

In October 1748, according to a statement by Beaven's son-in-law, London merchant Josiah Knight[14], Beaven had "heard, in some public house near Exchange, that the King of Spain had set up a manufacture of cloth in Madrid". Beaven had followed this up with the Spanish Legation in London who told him that if he would undertake to teach his trade in Spain he could have £500 a year and the work-people he took with him would be paid £50 a year each. In addition Beaven would have £500 for his expenses and a house to live in, free exercise of his religion and protection against molestation. He was to go for seven years certain and after that would be free to stay or go as he wished. Beaven found the offer interesting and asked one Joseph Earle to go with him.

Knight continues: "On November 17 (1748) my poor father set out for Melksham to see what he could do with his creditors in order to get a certificate. Stayed till about the middle of January to no purpose. He then went to a friend of mine at Exeter who got him a lodging at Stacross close by the seaside. Efforts were still being made to get a certificate signed."

At Exeter Beaven boarded the *Mayflower*, then on a voyage to London. In London he stayed at Knight's house before returning to Melksham to try once again to persuade his creditors to sign a certificate of release. Hearing that there were two bailiffs in wait for him he fled over the river to catch the stage coach for Bristol. On the way to the coach he was robbed.

On 20 March 1749 we find Beaven in Bristol, getting ready to set off for Spain by way of London. He furnishes one John Fry with a pair of shoes, gives him 4s.6d. to make his way to London (evidently on foot) and arranges to meet him there at Josiah Knight's house. Fry was said to have told his friends at Melksham that he was going to Spain with Beaven and was to have £10 a year.

Beaven's creditors and his fellow-clothiers were relentless. They not only firmly refused to agree to any arrangement by which he could obtain his discharge but tried to terrify him with threats of what the law might do to him — including hanging! (Though hanging was out of the question a spell in a debtor's prison was a real possibility; as we have seen he was dodging the bailiffs). They argued that a man who was willing to teach foreign competitors English skills was a traitor and they prevailed upon Zachariah Shrapnel[15] of Midway Manor, Bradford on Avon, leading clothier and landowner, to raise the matter at the highest level.

Shrapnel accordingly, "on behalf of the clothiers and gentlemen of Melksham", on 5 August 1749 wrote to a Mr Dennys de Berdt, evidently a very senior official, requesting that the attention of the Secretary of State be drawn to what he called Beaven's "infamous scheme" to take "many artificers in the clothing trade" and set up in Spain.

Berdt showed the letter to the Duke of Bedford, who showed it to the king, and warrants were issued to seize Beaven and the two men, Earle and Fry, whom he was intending to take to Spain with him.

Beaven succeeded in getting away to Spain, either in late 1749 or early 1750. and set up in business at San Fernando, near Madrid, He took with him the two skilled English clothworkers. But it was not long before he wanted to return home. Perversely his enemies now tried to stop him coming back. A group of Melksham Quaker clothiers[16] tried to help him. In a letter dated 3 September 1750 they appealed to their fellow-clothiers to withdraw their objections to his return, but their efforts were in vain, the London clothiers in particular, for no obvious reason, being unwilling to help. But they had better luck with the Law Officers of the Crown, obtaining from them a statement that should he return to England, no action would be taken to prosecute him provided he gave sureties to stay.

On 29 July 1751 Beaven informed the British representative in Madrid that he wished to return to England. He sought employment or a pension of £300 a year and protection from his creditors. Their response does not seem to be on record.

We hear no more of Thomas III in the minutes, nor does his name appear in the index of births and burials[17] in the Quaker collection in the Wiltshire Record Office. The last time he took part in local Quaker affairs seems to have been Quarterly Meeting on 4 November 1747, which must have been shortly before he went broke. But he may have been the Thomas Beaven mentioned in a deed of 1777. Among new trustees of the Melksham Friends meeting-house property appointed in that year were brothers John, Samuel and Thomas Beaven the Younger, sons of Thomas Beaven "late of Melksham, now of Granton" (*see* Appendix H). If so he would then be 79 and has exiled himself to Somerset. It sounds possible. On the other hand the name and description appear again in 1790, when he would have been 92. So that that Thomas may have been Thomas IV, born 1720 or even a later one. The Thomas Beavens did tend to abound. See Appendix H for trustee Thomas Beaven, gentleman, living at Bruton in 1825.

One would like to know more about the circumstances surrounding this sad story. Thomas III had in happier days given good service to the Society of Friends, but seems to have received little support when he needed it. Many of his friends and relations were well-off. Were his debts so enormous that they could not have helped him out? From what little we do know, Melksham Friends' treatment of him was uncharacteristically shabby, particularly when we compare it with their charitable forbearance towards his father (Thomas II) forty years before. Why? They could have saved themselves much embarrassment had they lent a helping hand.

Could it have been that they were themselves hard-up? Times were difficult in the clothing industry. What had happened to the old Quaker solidarity? It may be significant that when in December 1744 Quarterly Meeting sought to raise £162 to pay off accumulated debts, although they kept the list open for two years, the sum received fell well short of what was needed, this is spite of the fact that they prepared a subscription list with the names of Friends to be asked to contribute and a space to record the amount each gave. The list shows that many addressed failed to respond, though, as stated above. Thomas III did, and generously[18].

NOTES

1. Thomas Story, Quaker minister, recorded in his journal that when he was in Devizes in 1722 (in the course of a preaching tour) he stayed the night with Roger.

Story (c1670-1742), lawyer turned Quaker minister, travelled widely "in the ministry" and kept a detailed, almost daily, record of his travels and the meetings he addressed. His journal was published by Isaac Thompson, Newcastle upon Tyne, in 1747.

2. We note that in 1712, for example, the vicar of Melksham (Bohun Fox) seized malt for unpaid tithe and church rate. A tithe impropriator (person who had acquired the right to collect tithe) seized barley.

3. In the library of Friends House London. The original was printed in London (by The Assigns of J. Bowle at the Bible in George-yard in Lombard Street) in 1723. The 1793 re-printing was by James Phillips, George-yard, Lombard Street. In 1813 William Alexander produced a pamphlet called *On Prayer* which was based on, and largely extracted from, Beaven's original. This was printed in York by Thomas Wilson and Sons, High Ousegate. Other religious writings by Beaven on record include:

> The agency of God and the Agency of Man co-working in the Salvation of Man. London 1727.

> The Truth and Excellency of the Gospel Dispensation briefly considered. London 1727. (Anonymous, but believed to be by Beaven).

> Supernatural influences necessary to Salvation being a Vindication of the four Propositions of Robert Barclay's Apology for the true Christian Divinity, in answer to Thomas Chubb's Treatise. London 1727 and Scripture Evidence defended, being a Review of the Controversy betwixt Thomas Chubb and Thomas Beaven. London 1728.

Robert Barclay's classic work *An Apology for the True Christian Divinity as the same is held forth and preached by the People in Scorn Called Quakers* was published in Latin in 1676 and in English in 1678. Thomas Chubb (1679-1747) was a leading Deist. Deists held that God existed but denied revelation and the authority of the Christian church; they believed that there was no divine providence governing the affairs of men. Beaven was clearly disputing at a high intellectual level.

4. "While [Penn] was at Melksham, a dispute was held between John Plympton, a Baptist, and John Clarke of Bradford on the part of the Quakers in the courtyard belonging to Thomas Beaven's house. The Baptist had challenged the Quakers to a public conference on five subjects: the Universality of Grace, Baptism, the Lord's Supper, Perfection and the Resurrection. Clarke is said to have answered the objections of Plympton notably: but Plympton would not allow it; and though the auditors were against him he continued to cavil on and would not be silenced. At length, evening coming on, William Penn rose, and, to use the words of a spectator 'breaking like a thunderstorm over his head in testimony to the people' who were numerous, concluded the dispute".

Thomas Clarkson: *Memories of the Life of William Penn.*

John Clarke was a leading Bradford on Avon and Lavington Monthly Meeting Friend. He was also a locally well-known and highly respected medical practitioner.

5. "Hat honour". Early Friends claimed that removal of the hat in deference was due only to the Almighty, namely when at prayer.

6. Distinctive language. The use of the second person singular when addressing an individual. The practice continues among Quakers in some parts of the United States of America.

7. By "Petty-coat Fathers" he presumably meant women ministers.

8. The allusion is to the words of the Jewish ruler Agrippa to the Apostle Paul: "Almost thou persuadest me to be a Christian" (Acts 26 v 28).

9. The printed pamphlets unfolding this sorry fracas, all in the library of Friends House, London, are as follows:-

i. Thomas Beaven's complaint against members of the Society of Friends and resignation, 1706. (The handwritten original has found its way into the British Library — item Add MS 34727, ff236/7).

ii. (i) above copied by Bohun Fox. Printed and sold by Benjamin Bragge at the Black Raven in Paternoster Row.

iii. *Thomas Beaven's Second Part in relation to the Quakers.* Bristol: printed by W.B. 1707

iv. *Thomas Beaven's Second Thoughts in relation to the Quakers.* Printed and sold by Benjamin Bragg at the Black Raven in Paternoster Row.

v. *Agrippa almost persuaded to be a Christian, or the Self-condemn'd Quaker, being a true Copy of the two Papers lately printed by THOMAS BEAVEN in relation to the Quakers with a Preface and some Reflections on the Last of them, Entituled, His Second Thoughts.* By Bohun Fox LL B Vicar of Melksham and late Fellow of New College., Oxon.

vi. *The High Priest of Melksham, his Reasonings, his Concessions and his Self-contradictions: Briefly examined in a Sober Vindication of a Paper entituled Second Thoughts, Relating to the Quakers being a reply to Bohun Fox's Agrippa &c.* London: J. Bowle in White-hart Court in Gracious Street, 1707.

vii. *Some Observations on the Controversie lately depending between Bohun Fox, Vicar of Melksham, and Thomas Beaven, Jnr.* London: J. Bowle, 1708.

10. Story recorded that at Cullompton he lodged overnight with Thomas Finnimore, "where, in the evening, there came Thomas Beaven from Melksham and several Friends with him; where he favoured us with the reading of his Manuscript, proving that Reason in Man and divine Truth, are distinct Things; on which Subject he

and I had sometimes discoursed before, as very necessary to be fully and plainly treated upon ..."

11. WRO 1699/115. They had been incurred over the previous twenty years, partly as a result of lawsuits defending the legality of Quaker marriages.

12. Wiltshire Archaeological and Natural History Society Cuttings Book 14.

13. QUAKERS AND BANKRUPTCY
It is surprising that Wiltshire Monthly Meeting minutes are silent about Beaven's failure.

Thrift and the work ethic have always informed the Religious Society of Friends. Up to the middle of the nineteenth century Quakers as much as anyone believed in the historic veracity of the Book of Genesis and the obligation to atone for Adam's transgression by toil. The success in business so often achieved by the industrious and thrifty encouraged the belief that failure amounted to moral short-coming. Thus to fail and leave creditors unpaid incurred censure from Monthly Meeting because the member concerned had not lived up to what the Society required of him or her.

Meetings were enjoined to keep an eye on this. A letter of 27.3.1675 from a General Meeting held in London advised

> That Friends and brethren in their respective Meetings
> watch over one another in the love of God and care of
> the Gospel particularly that none trade beyond their
> ability nor stretch beyond their compass ...

In the eighteenth and nineteenth centuries bankruptcy usually incurred formal disownment. A classic instance is the case of Joseph Fry, (Melksham Friend Rachel Fowler's brother-in-law, husband of Elizabeth Fry, the prison reformer) who was disowned by his Meeting when the bank of which he was head failed in the course of the depression which followed the Napoleonic Wars.

In 1883 Melksham ironmonger Henry Simpson became insolvent with unpaid debts of some £6,000 (a very substantial sum in the days when a man could be declared bankrupt for a debt of £50). The Friends appointed by Monthly Meeting to go into the matter reported laxity in the keeping of accounts; failure to balance books or take stock for several years; undesirable habits and associations involving neglect of the business; and "considerable laxity" in his management of Quaker trust funds. North Somerset and Wiltshire Monthly Meeting recorded strong disapproval; Minute 6 of their meeting in November 1883 expressed regret that "Henry Simpson's failure has not only brought discredit on a name and family held heretofore in high esteem but has also entailed reproach upon our religious society". Surprisingly, they did not disown him.

In 1892 two bankrupt Wiltshire Quakers were dealt with as follows:-

North Somerset and Wiltshire Monthly Meeting held 13th 4th month 1892.

Minute 3. It is after careful consideration and feelings of deep regret that the Monthly Meeting has arrived at the decision that they cannot retain Walter James Wood's name on the list of members...It is felt that the circumstances which preceded and accompanied Walter Wood's insolvency are such that this Meeting cannot well adopt any other course ... they hope that this painful experience will impress upon his mind that every violation of the law of strict integrity brings upon the offender unhappiness in the world and if not truly repented of in the world to come...

Thomas Baker's failure...we feel it right to express our censure on his having incurred debts with considerable uncertainty in the prospect of their liquidation and that at an early period of his difficulties he did not take counsel with some Friends as to his financial position. This Meeting desires always to feel a tender solicitude towards those who engage in vocal exercises in our Meetings for Worship or who take part in temperance or other moral reforms. Yet they are of opinion that Thomas Baker would have acted wisely in keeping these things in abeyance while his outward affairs were in such a state as to result in a reproach on our Christian professions. We are glad that he admits his moral responsibility to pay his debts in full and hope that his future circumstances will enable him to do so.

14. Josiah Knight had married Beaven's daughter Mary in 1742. They lived in Token House Yard, in the City of London.

15. Zachariah was the father of General Henry Shrapnel who invented the exploding "shrapnel" shell.

16. Will Timbrell, Joseph Lanham Junior, Sam Rutty, James Moore, Paul Newman and Jon Rutty.

17. WRO 854/1.

18. Subscription list 1744 contained in file of miscellaneous papers at WRO 1699/115. See also note 1 to Chapter 8 (i).

(iii) THE RUTTYS

John Rutty (1671-1726) we have already met in connexion with his encounters with the vicar over non-payment of tithe and with the establishment of the Quaker school. He came of a Melksham family which went back to the early 1400s[1]. The earliest Melksham Rutty we know of was Thomas, born in 1540, John Rutty's great-great grandfather. John joined the Society of Friends in 1692, the first of the family to do so.

John was a maltster by trade. The records show him to have been of very high standing in the Quaker community, solicitous on behalf of impoverished Friends, dedicated to the Society and regularly called upon to perform duties for it. Among other things he audited accounts, represented his Meeting at monthly, quarterly and yearly meetings and acted as mediator and peacemaker when differences arose. His house was regularly used for Quaker business meetings. He was well-to-do, easily able to support the cost of sending a son to university abroad.

But there was one area in which his service frequently fell short. He was, for a number of years from July 1712, clerk of Lavington Monthly Meeting, but the Meeting suffered from their clerk's chronic forgetfulness. Time and time again he turned up without the minute-book, making it difficult for the meeting to proceed. In June 1714 the Meeting formally required him to minute their reprimand:

> This Meeting desires our Clerk to take more care
> for the future yt we may not be disappointed in
> our Business.

In June the following year he again forgot and a minute of reprimand was again formally recorded.

At the very next meeting there was not only no minute-book but no John Rutty either. The Meeting was now losing patience and John Gye was deputed to ask him why he was serving

Friends so. Rutty apologised to the Meeting, which recorded that it desired "it may not happen so no more". But it did — in November.

And so it went on, year after year, reprimand and apology until John handed over to his son Samuel shortly after a minute of 10 February 1721:

> Forasmuch as our Book has been neglected to be brought to this Meeting severall Times it's proposed yt we chuse a new Clark.

The change may or may not have been an improvement. The fact that in October 1716 Samuel had had to admit to Monthly Meeting that documents in his care had been consumed by rats must surely have given rise to some misgivings.

That Friends had put up with John Rutty's forgetfulness so long was a tribute to his character and outstanding qualities in other fields, and, of course, to their tolerance. Bearing in mind that to get to Monthly Meeting they will have had to journey over unpaved ways for up to twenty miles, some on horseback some on foot, their forbearance is remarkable. There was apparently not the slightest rancour on either side and Rutty continued to serve the Meeting in various capacities to within a few days of his death on 31 October 1726.

Samuel Rutty (1695-1762), grocer and clothier, married, in 1722, Mary Tyler of Lavington. Their marriage was a happy one as, indeed, were most Quaker marriages in the days when they had to have the specific approval of the Society if the parties were to remain in membership. Four affectionate letters from Samuel to Mary have survived. They are summarised at Appendix F.

Samuel and Mary's daughter Katherine (1727-62) married, in 1753, Thomas Fowler (1730-83). Thereafter the Fowler family lived and thrived in Melksham for more than two and a half centuries. Their story is told in my next chapter.

John (1698-1775), Samuel's brother[2], became Dr John Rutty MD, the distinguished eighteenth century physician. His earliest education was almost certainly at the Melksham Quaker school. As a brilliant pupil he will in due course have outstripped its scope and been sent elsewhere. Many years later[3] he recalled his first school with approval. It was, he wrote, "a seminary ... not only of learning but of religion". There he "received a little of the heavenly fire". But in adolescence he was sent elsewhere and found himself "among aliens" where he "lived without God".

At age 20 he lodged for two years with a Quaker family and re-entered the Quaker fold. "Some inclination to marriage" was "over-ruled by a secret hand". At 22 he moved to London. Then, barred by his religious affiliation from the English universities he entered the University of Leyden to read for his medical degree. Although he will have chosen Leyden because of the well-established Quaker community there[4] his stay in Holland was, he wrote, "all nature and physic, no grace ...". He was now anxious to get on in the world, possessing, as he said, but slender private means.

The *Album Studiosum* of the University of Leyden records that he was awarded his doctorate on 14 March 1722. (It was for a thesis on diarrhoea.) He seems to have returned to England intending to practise here. But in July 1724 he is back in Melksham briefly before setting off for Dublin to try his hand there. Meeting at Melksham that month Friends of Lavington Monthly Meeting composed a charming letter of introduction to Dublin Friends:

> From the Men's Monthly Meeting held at Melksham
> in the County of Wilts in the Kingdom of Great
> Brittain 10th of the 5th Month 1724
> To the Men's Monthly Meeting in the City of Dublin
> in the Kingdom of Ireland

Dear Friends

Our well beloved ingenuous Friend John Rutty Doctor of Physick having desired a certificate to you from our Monthly Meeting on account of his design to settle among you if business shall encourage him and you approve thereof

Wee do therefore accordingly certify you that as wee esteem him a man well learn'd in the languages & very understanding in physick so his behaviour and conversation hath been sober and orderly among us and wee know not but he is clear from all women respecting marriage

Wherefore commending him to your regard and favour hopeing if he settles with you he may be blessed with the success and service among you & your neighbours as his capacity indefatigable diligence and long studys seems to promise wee conclude with the salutation of our dear love.

Your Friends and Brethren in the blessed truth signed by order & in behalf of our sd Meeting by

> *Thomas Beaven Senior*
> *John Clarke*
> *Jos Hull*
> *James Matravers*
> *James Band*
> *Paul Newman Jun.*
> *Edwd Gye*

John Clarke, who as Monthly Meeting clerk will have originated the letter, himself a medical practitioner, doubtless thoroughly approved of the young Doctor Rutty[5].

Although Rutty did not return to Melksham to live he kept in touch with his family and with Friends there and doubtless visited from time to time. Thomas Fowler (1730-1783), his nephew by marriage, was an executor of his will. But Dublin was where his home and Quaker community were from 1724.

Between 1742 and 1775, the year he died, he published a number of scholarly works on medical matters as well as a history of Quakers in Ireland and a natural history of the county of Dublin. His last work, a Latin treatise called *Materia Medica Antiqua et Nova*, published in Rotterdam in 1775, had been 40 years in the writing. It is, I believe, to this day considered a classic and still useful work of reference[6].

John Rutty was much influenced by the Quietism[7] which developed in the Society during his lifetime. This influence found expression in the "Spiritual Diary" which he kept from 1753 until his death in 1775. Quietist self-denigration predominates but there is also in it something of the confessional. A member of another persuasion would have unburdened himself to a priest; Rutty made his confession to what Quakers would call "that of God" in himself and in his fellows. Doubtless it was for this reason that he made provision in his will for its publication after his death "without delay and without alteration or amendment". Fifty copies were duly printed, thirty for London Yearly Meeting, ten for Dublin Meeting and ten for Wiltshire Friends.

The work was probably read widely within the Society of Friends at the time but non-Quakers would be puzzled by it. Dr Samuel Johnson's biographer James Boswell recorded that the account of it which appeared in the press afforded Johnson some amusement and the opportunity to soliloquise on why men keep diaries[8].

Whenever Methodist John Wesley visited Dublin, Rutty was his medical adviser. Despite temperamental and religious differences, the two were clearly firm friends. In his journal Wesley records on 6 April 1775 his very last visit to that "venerable Quaker, now tottering over the grave" but "clear in his understanding, full of faith and love, and patiently waiting till his change should come"[9].

The words were a fitting final tribute to a great and saintly man.

There were Ruttys in Melksham Quaker Meeting until the beginning of the nineteenth century. In the Quaker records we find the names of

> Clare and Hannah (1703-77),
> Jonathan and Hannah, daughter of Samuel Sanger
> (died June 1768),
> Esther (1768-1797),
> Richard (1733-1807) "buried Mary Marshman's
> burial ground at Shaw",
> Martha, spinster (1744-1809),
> John and Mary (fl.1784).

Thereafter the name disappears from the Quaker records to reappear in Methodist ones; in June 1804 Samuel Rutty is named as an applicant in the registration certificate for the Methodist chapel[10]. The Henry Rutty (fl.1706) who was a tithe impropriator (lay owner) whom we find distraining John Rutty's goods (*see* chapter 5 -Tithe Testimony) may well have been a kinsman. In the 1660s there was the Reverend Thomas Rutty who lived in Seend and was preaching nonconformity at Calne in 1669[11].

In 1766 there was in Keevil Thomas Rutty, innkeeper, and in 1816 a descendant of his, David Rutty, maltster. In 1817 there were in Seend John and James Rutty, cordwainers[12].

NOTES

1. According to the Fowler family history, privately printed in 1891 (see Bibliography).

2. Dr John Rutty's father was not, as stated in the *Dictionary of National Biography*, Richard — that was the name of his grandfather. The Fowler family history confirms this.

3. In his "Spiritual diary".

4. He was not the first English Quaker medical student to choose Leyden. Michael Lee Dicker (1694-1752 had taken his MD there only a year or two before Rutty went up. (Dicker later became physician at the Royal Devon and Exeter Hospital).

5. From quite early in the history of the movement there were Wiltshire Quakers who took up medicine as a career. John Clarke's son followed in his father's profession at Bradford on Avon and a few years later we meet Joseph Fry (1730/89) of Sutton Benger, who, however, abandoned a lucrative medical practice in Bristol to pursue an even more lucrative one in business there as a manufacturer of chocolate. In Melksham Meeting itself we find surgeon Simon Shewring (died 1721), apothecary Samuel Shurmer (fl. 1739), William Cookworthy, surgeon (1731-1786) and William Tully Simpson (1768-1808) who married Maria Gundry (1764-1843) of Calne in 1793 and moved to Melksham in 1796 to practise there as a physician till his death 12 years later.

6. Published works of Dr.John Rutty:

(a) *An account of experiments on Joanna Stephen's medicine for the stone.* London 1742.
(b) *A methodical analysis of mineral waters.* London 1757.
(c) *A history of the rise and progress of the people called Quakers in Ireland from 1653 to 1751.*
(d) *The analysis of milk.* Dublin 1762.
(e) *The weather and seasons in Dublin for 40 years.* 1770. (It deals

with diseases prevalent during that period).
(f) *A natural history of the county of Dublin.*   1772.
(g) *Materia medica antiqua et nova.*   Rotterdam 1775.

7. Quietism, a somewhat extreme form of mysticism, was new to eighteenth century Friends but had been known elsewhere in the Christian church for some time. It stemmed from the writings of the Spaniard Miguel de Molinos (1640-1697) who held that the road to perfection lay only through total annihilation of the will and abandonment of the self to God. It started to develop among Quakers both here and in America from about 1725 and remained an influence up to a century later.

8. *The Life of Samuel Johnson* by James Boswell. Boswell wrote:

> He was much diverted with an article which I showed him in the Critical Review of this year, giving an extract of a curious publication entitled *A Spiritual Diary and Soliloquies by John Rutty MD"*. Dr. Rutty was one of the people called Quakers, a physician of some eminence in Dublin, and author of several works. This diary, which was kept from 1753 to 1775, the year in which he died, and was now published in two volumes octave, exhibited in the simplicity of his heart, a minute and honest register of the state of his mind; which, though frequently laughable enough, was not more so than the history of many men would be, if recorded with equal fairness.

The following specimens were extracted by the Reviewers:

> "Tenth month, 1753.

> 23. Indulgence in bed an hour too long.

> Twelfth month, 17. An hypochondriac conubilation from wind and indigestion.

Ninth month, 28. An over-dose of whisky.

29. A dull cross choleric day.

First month 1757, 22. A little swinish at dinner and repast.

31.Dogged on provocation.

Second month, 5. Very dogged and snappish.

14. Snappish on fasting.

26. Cursed snappishness to those under me, on a bodily indisposition.

Third month, 11. On a provocation, exercised a dumb resentment for two days, instead of scolding.

22. Scolded too vehemently.

23. Dogged again.

Fourth month, 29. Mechanically and sinfully dogged."

Johnson laughed heartily at this good Quietist's self-condemning minutes; particularly at his mentioning with such serious regret, occasional instances of "swinishness" in eating, and "doggedness of temper".

9. *Journal* of John Wesley vol 4, page 40.

10. *Wiltshire Meeting House certificates 1689-1852* - John Chandler, Wilts Record Society (quoting WRO D1/2/29).

11. *Victoria County History* vol 7, quoting G. Lyon Turner: Original records of early Nonconformity.

12. Edward Bradby: *Seend, a Wiltshire Village* (1983).

(iv) THE FOWLERS[1]

Old Style:

> *Man, to the plough;*
> *Wife, to the cow;*
> *Girl, to the yarn;*
> *Boy, to the barn,*
>
> *And your rent will be netted.*

New style:

> *Man, Tally Ho;*
> *Miss, piano;*
> *Wife, silk and satin;*
> *Boy, Greek and Latin,*
>
> *And you'll all be Gazetted.*

Verses written in 1843

The rise of the Fowler family of Melksham from modest respectability to wealth and social standing reaching well beyond their immediate neighbourhood reflected current changes in English society generally. But it exemplifies, too, what was characteristic of the Religious Society of Friends in the eighteenth and nineteenth centuries. With them it was writ large. The rule that both parties in marriage must be members made for a family network which extended throughout the British Isles. Where better to seek a spouse than at the many Quaker gatherings and meetings for worship which took place throughout the year?

And where better to seek a business partner or to deploy

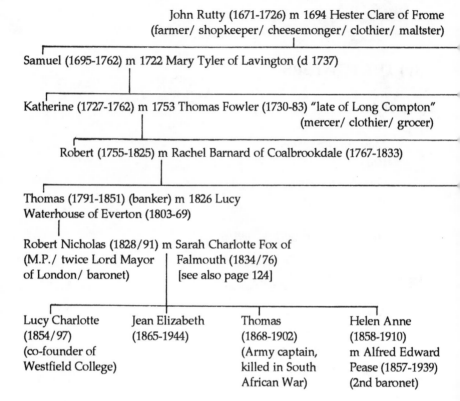

John Rutty (1671-1726) m 1694 Hester Clare of Frome
(farmer/ shopkeeper/ cheesemonger/ clothier/ maltster)

Samuel (1695-1762) m 1722 Mary Tyler of Lavington (d 1737)

Katherine (1727-1762) m 1753 Thomas Fowler (1730-83) "late of Long Compton"
(mercer/ clothier/ grocer)

Robert (1755-1825) m Rachel Barnard of Coalbrookdale (1767-1833)

Thomas (1791-1851) (banker) m 1826 Lucy
Waterhouse of Everton (1803-69)

Robert Nicholas (1828/91) m Sarah Charlotte Fox of
(M.P./ twice Lord Mayor | Falmouth (1834/76)
of London/ baronet) | [see also page 124]

Lucy Charlotte (1854/97) (co-founder of Westfield College) — Jean Elizabeth (1865-1944) — Thomas (1868-1902) (Army captain, killed in South African War) — Helen Anne (1858-1910) m Alfred Edward Pease (1857-1939) (2nd baronet)

Henry (1823/80) m 1848 Anne Ford Barclay
m 1848 (tea dealer (1822-1913)
and stove manufac- Recorded minister,
turer in partnership temperance
with brother Robert. advocate, Father
At death the banker. Direct
'gentleman' descendant of Robt.
Barclay (1648/90)
author of the *Apology*

Robert (1825-88)
(manufacturer in
partnership with
brother Henry)

John (1826-64)
(steam plough
inventor)

William Henry (1815/89) m (1839) Priscilla Gurney
(banker/ M.P.)

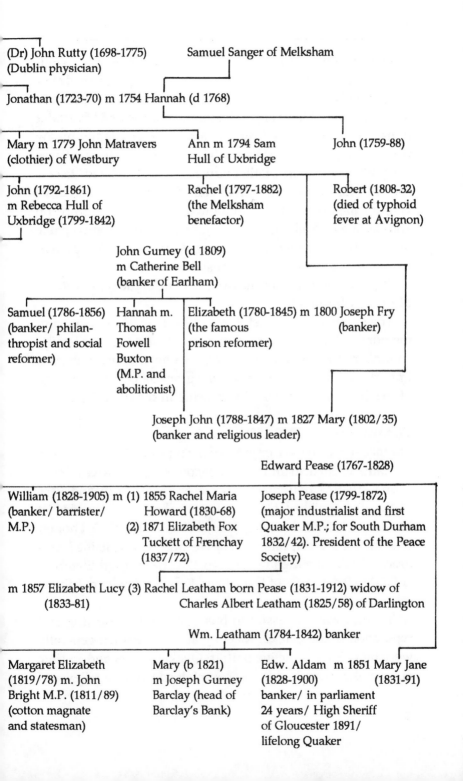

(Dr) John Rutty (1698-1775)   Samuel Sanger of Melksham
(Dublin physician)

Jonathan (1723-70) m 1754 Hannah (d 1768)

Mary m 1779 John Matravers   Ann m 1794 Sam   John (1759-88)
(clothier) of Westbury   Hull of Uxbridge

John (1792-1861)   Rachel (1797-1882)   Robert (1808-32)
m Rebecca Hull of   (the Melksham   (died of typhoid
Uxbridge (1799-1842)   benefactor)   fever at Avignon)

                 John Gurney (d 1809)
                 m Catherine Bell
                 (banker of Earlham)

Samuel (1786-1856)   Hannah m.   Elizabeth (1780-1845) m 1800 Joseph Fry
(banker/ philan-   Thomas   (the famous   (banker)
thropist and social Fowell   prison reformer)
reformer)   Buxton
                     (M.P. and
                     abolitionist)

                 Joseph John (1788-1847) m 1827 Mary (1802/35)
                 (banker and religious leader)

                              Edward Pease (1767-1828)

William (1828-1905) m (1) 1855 Rachel Maria   Joseph Pease (1799-1872)
(banker/ barrister/   Howard (1830-68) (major industrialist and first
M.P.)   (2) 1871 Elizabeth Fox   Quaker M.P.; for South Durham
                              Tuckett of Frenchay 1832/42). President of the Peace
                              (1837/72)   Society)

m 1857 Elizabeth Lucy (3) Rachel Leatham born Pease (1831-1912) widow of
        (1833-81)   Charles Albert Leatham (1825/58) of Darlington

                 Wm. Leatham (1784-1842) banker

Margaret Elizabeth   Mary (b 1821)   Edw. Aldam m 1851 Mary Jane
(1819/78) m. John   m Joseph Gurney   (1828-1900)   (1831-91)
Bright M.P. (1811/89)   Barclay (head of   banker/ in parliament
(cotton magnate   Barclay's Bank)   24 years/ High Sheriff
and statesman)   of Gloucester 1891/
                                              lifelong Quaker

capital? When John Fowler (1826-1864), the celebrated engineer and inventor wanted help with the design of his drain-plough and other experimental devices he naturally turned to fellow Quakers Albert Fry of Bristol and Ransomes &May (later Ransomes & Sims) of Ipswich. John Fowler's father-in-law through his marriage to Elizabeth Lucy Pease was Joseph Pease MP (1799-1872), whose father Edward (1767-1828) had "talent-spotted" George Stephenson in 1821, financed his locomotive venture and later had him appointed engineer to the Stockton and Darlington Railway. So when John Fowler needed a capable manufacturer for his prize-winning steam-plough Joseph was easily able to persuade Stephenson to do it for him.

The genealogical table illustrates some of the ramifications of the Fowler family.

The eponymous Rachel Fowler Centre in Melksham commemorates but one member of a remarkable Quaker family, a number of whose members achieved much more than local importance. Rachel Fowler was the granddaughter of the first of the Quaker Fowler family to settle in the town. This was

Thomas Fowler (1730-1783)

Thomas seems to have originated at Shipston, Worcestershire. He came to Melksham from Longcompton, Warwickshire to court Catherine, daughter of Samuel and Mary Rutty and niece of the distinguished Dr John Rutty. They were married at Melksham Friends Meeting House in September 1753. Thomas was then a mercer; later (1777) we find him described as a grocer. Catherine died in 1762. In 1765 he married Elizabeth (1737-1787) daughter of Daniel and Rebecca Fowler of Minchinhampton.

Thomas was successful in business and his standing and reputation in the Quaker Meeting and in the town generally were high. He was active both in Quaker affairs and in civic ones; in the latter field it was complained that as a reliever of the poor he was more generous with public funds than he need be!

Robert Fowler (1755-1825)

Thomas Fowler's son Robert (philanthropist Rachel Fowler's father) attended first the Quaker school, now removed to Pickwick, to be thoroughly grounded by Thomas Bennet in the three Rs plus Latin and Greek. (He will have been a contemporary of Richard Reynolds there, being within a few months the same age). He then went on to a school at Worcester. As was usual in those days the classics were paramount and at neither establishment were modern languages taught. Robert's Latin was good and stayed with him; but he regretted his lack of French when, towards the end of his life, having developed an interest in France he made it his business to travel there "under concern".

At 15 Robert left school to join the family business which thirteen years later he inherited. In August 1790, aged 35, he married Rachel Barnard, youngest daughter of John and Hannah Barnard (born Wilson) of Upper Thorpe, near Sheffield.

Robert inherited his father's business acumen and shared his religious attitudes. In business he prospered to the extent that at his death in 1825 the Quaker register of burials accords him the status of gentleman. A study of the Quaker register[2] of goods distrained in respect of unpaid tithes and church-rate shows that he had widened the family business interests to include drapery (Irish linen taken in 1793), stationery (16 reams of paper taken in 1882) and farming at Box (wheat taken by the rector there in 1794), all for substantial amounts.

Fowler family tradition has it that it was of him that the poet George Crabbe (vicar at St. James's Church, Trowbridge from 1814 to 1832) wrote the lines:

Dealer in hops, and malt and coals and corn
And like his father he was merchant born.

He was, besides, senior partner in the firm of Fowler and Phillips, one of the two Melksham banks of the day.[3]

For many years the family business had conducted a lucrative trade supplying local inns with spirits. At some time after 1795 (the records show that in that year rum and brandy were still being seized in respect of unpaid tithe), Robert gave up this side of the business as inconsistent with the profession of religion. In later years he is said to have often referred with thankfulness to the blessings he believed he had received from this sacrifice. It was at the time of the Napoleonic Wars, and local cynics are said to have observed that one of these blessings was that he was no longer obliged to undertake the billetting of soldiers as he had been as the holder of a liquor licence. Given Robert's strong pacifist views there may have been an element of truth in this. The Quaker records of tithe restraints reveal that the trade resumed later on, doubtless when Robert, in order to pursue his Quakerly concerns, relinquished management to sons Thomas and John.

In 1799 Robert was appointed a "recorded minister" while attending Yearly Meeting in Dublin. In the same year the family moved out of the town itself, having bought a house and land at Gastard which they called Elm Grove (later to be the site of the present Gastard House).

While travelling "in the ministry" in Cumberland Robert became aware how poorly educated were the less affluent Friends there and came in consequence to play an important part in the establishment of the Quaker school at Wigton. An enthusiast for education for all classes he tried hard to get established a school for the poor in Melksham. He selected a plot of land for the purpose but got no support and had to drop the idea, though after his death a school for boys and girls was erected on the spot he had chosen.

A serious illness in 1813 caused him to ponder the unwisdom of too great attachment to the accumulation of wealth. Leaving his two sons Thomas and John in charge of the family business Robert thereafter dedicated himself largely to Quaker affairs, travelling much "in the ministry", including three visits to Ireland.

In the 1780s British Friends had been delighted to discover that from about 1716 at Congénies, Calvisson and other towns and villages in southern France groups of French Protestants had quite independently adopted attitudes and practices indistinguishable from their own. This French brand of Quakerism stemmed from the persecution of the Huguenots which had followed the revocation of the Edict of Nantes. Having made the discovery, British Friends were keen to establish links and maintain them; and it will have been this that inspired Robert Fowler to visit them.

The defeat of the French army at Waterloo in 1815 put an end to the long years of war and made the resumption of contacts possible. Apart from the Quaker connexion British Friends saw the French as largely without religion and greatly in need of it. Robert entered into this with enthusiasm. From the family memoir (*see* Note 1) we learn that in the Spring of 1823, now aged 68 and within two years of his death, he set off for France. He took with him Josiah Forster and a nephew "I.F.H" (in the memoir members of near family are always referred to by their initials. I F H will have been the son of Robert's sister Ann, married to Samuel Hull of Uxbridge).

With no French — though presumably Josiah Forster and possibly the nephew had some — it was, for Robert, very much an act of faith. But it seems to have seen him through. Before setting off for the south to visit the French Quakers there — by this time the English ones had, in a sense, adopted them — he stayed six weeks in Paris where they set up a depot for

Quaker books at the house of a saddler in the Rue Castiglione.

A measure of the good reputation which British Quakers had now acquired in France (in part at least through the writings of Voltaire[4]) was that he was politely received by those in authority. With Forster he called in turn on each of three ministers of state respectively responsible for the three matters about which he was most concerned: that the scriptures should be allowed to circulate freely in France, that the Sabbath should be properly observed and that the continuance of peace should be promoted.

From Paris the little party travelled south to Congénies where he and "S.C." (evidently another of his relations) spent two weeks visiting most of the Quaker families in the vicinity before returning home to Melksham.

The following year Robert went back to France taking with him Rachel and some members of his family. There at the same time was Edward Pease (1767-1858) with whom he joined forces to promote a shared concern that the slave trade, abolished in Britain in 1808, should cease everywhere.

In the autumn Robert became ill and the party had to return home. A month in Bath, which failed to effect any improvement, was followed by a short spell at Clifton, where he seemed to rally. Back at Melksham decline resumed and the end came in April 1825.

Robert was highly respected in the town and the funeral at the Friends Meeting House was an outstanding event. Although himself a leader in a movement which rejected the tenets of the Church of England he was nevertheless on excellent terms with the Anglican clergy and with members of other religious denominations. The paradox of tithes and church-rate taken under duress and faithfully recorded as "sufferings" do not seem to have affected relationships at all; the *Devizes Gazette* of 5 May 1825 commented that among the "vast concourse" present at his funeral at the meeting-house in King Street were several clergymen of the Church of England.

Rachel Fowler I (1767-1833)

Rachel survived her husband Robert by eight years. We know something about her life from material privately printed in Norwich in 1838, probably at the behest of the Gurney in-laws, for circulation among other members of a numerous family[5]. She went to school at Kendal and was a studious pupil; in later life she was a keen reader.

She was a recorded minister and, so far as the claims of household and children permitted, from 1795 travelled "in the ministry". In that year we find her, accompanied by her friend Anne Alexander, visiting first Norfolk and Suffolk then the Channel Islands. On Sark we find her addressing "knitting women" who spoke no English and whose tongue she did not understand and being concerned about their dire poverty. She later travelled in Scotland.

After Robert's death she spent little time at Elm Grove, preferring to stay with members of her family, sometimes at Tottenham but most of the time at Melksham with her son John. In the autumn of 1830, then aged 63, she suffered an injury to her right side when alighting from her pony-chair (two-wheeled carriage). The injury seemed slight at the time but soon developed into a serious permanent disability; the efforts of her medical advisers notwithstanding, her right hand and arm became paralysed and caused her acute pain. The death of her son Robert at Avignon in 1832 at the age of 24 was a bitter blow and doubtless hastened her own demise in the following year.

John Fowler (1792-1861)

John, second son of Robert and Rachel, remained a Melksham Quaker. He and his brother Thomas managed the family grocery business while their father was away in France and elsewhere and took over alone when Thomas left Melksham for London in 1822. From 1816 he had been farming on his own account. The records show that in that year the church authorities seized from him wheat, peas, a cow and calf and four pigs to the value in total of £67.6s. Similar distraints were levied in subsequent years.

Later on there were distraints of hops, spirits (1824) and cheese (1828) in substantial amounts, from which it is clear that he had taken charge of the grocery business and tea and wine merchants' trade and carried it on after his father's death in 1825. But he clearly enjoyed most the farm and being in the open air; a keen horseman he was out riding against advice the very day of his death. Throughout his life he was active in the Melksham Meeting as was his wife Rebecca, born Hull, whom he married in 1822. He was a recorded minister.

Thomas Fowler (1791-1851)
John's brother Thomas, as well as helping in their father's business, farmed for a while at Rudloe. But at the age of 31 he was made a partner in William Holt's Bank, (to be re-named Drewett and Fowler), in London, and spent the rest of his life there. In 1826 he married Lucy Waterhouse, of Everton, Liverpool, a lady tireless in good works, well suited to the Fowler family tradition.

The sophistication of life as a City of London banker does not seem to have affected Thomas's way of life as a Quaker, probably because there were many of that persuasion there. So quiet was Quaker Meeting, quipped a wag, that one could hear there the movement of shares. Thomas is known to have been a kindly and generous man who did not spare himself in efforts to relieve poverty and hardship wherever it was to be found. He was particularly active during the distress in Lancashire in 1842 and in Ireland during the potato famine of 1846/7.

Robert Fowler (1808-1832)

Robert and Rachel's third son Robert was not cast in the typical Fowler mould. A place at the age of 16 in the counting-house of William Ridgeway in Bristol was not a bit to his liking; the offer of a post in the Saffron Walden branch with a view to partnership was no better received. Announcing that he would enjoy his fortune while he was young he took off for foreign parts. But he seems to have retained his Quaker links; we hear of him joining with his sister and other Friends in Quaker activities in Paris in 1829. On 13 November 1832 he died of typhoid fever while staying at the Hotel d'Europe, Avignon.

Rachel Fowler II (1797-1882)

Robert and Rachel's elder daughter Rachel is the member of the Fowler family whose name is best remembered in Melksham. As a young girl she was studious and a keen walker, an interesting conversationalist, but dour. A budding romance with a local curate could not blossom, blighted as it was by the tyrannical rigidity of the Quaker rules of the day forbidding marriage to a non-member on pain of expulsion. She was to live to see the rule abolished (in 1859). But for poor Rachel in her young day there was only the stark choice between the object of her affections and her beloved Society of Friends.[6]

So Rachel remained a spinster and gradually slipped into the role of archetypal maiden aunt, dispensing goodies to her many nephews and nieces and generally spoiling them all. There were compensations for her. Through the family network she enjoyed friendship with many of the good and great of the day. A particularly stimulating period in her life followed her sister Mary's death in 1835, when, for a few years, she went to keep house at Earlham for her brother-in-law the famous Joseph John Gurney (1788-1847), banker, religious leader and proponent of reform in the Society of Friends. There she rubbed shoulders with Joseph John's sisters, Elizabeth Fry, prison

Above: *Rachel Fowler (1797 - 1882)*
Opposite above: *The New Hall, Market Place, Melksham, built at Rachel Fowler's expense in 1877 and presented by her to the town as a lecture hall and reading-room.*
Opposite below: *The Retreat, The City, Melksham. Founded by Rachel Fowler as almshouses for poor widows and spinsters now, in changed times, adopted as housing for both sexes.*

An artist's impression of the building in Bank Street, Melksham, as it probably was in the lifetime of Rachel Fowler, the Melksham benefactress. The whole building is likely to have belonged to Rachel's parents Robert and Rachel before they moved to Elm Grove, Gastard. Later on it was divided into three, then four, separate dwellings. Rachel Fowler, who inherited from her parents, lived relatively modestly (considering her very ample means) in the one at the north end (to the right of the picture)

reformer, and Hannah, who had become Lady Buxton through her marriage with Sir Thomas Fawell Buxton, a leading opponent of the slave trade, and many other distinguished relations and in-laws with whom she seems to have been on equal intellectual and educational terms. Her father Robert, regretting his own ignorance of living foreign tongues, had made sure that Rachel had, as well as Latin, French and Italian. She was also well-read in the contemporary English poets.

Like her father Robert, Rachel got on well with the local clergy and was on particularly good terms with the vicar. But, again like her father, she stuck by the Quaker rules and dutifully refused to pay church-rate or vicarial tithe. Routinely she underwent distraint of her goods, in 1855, for example, silver spoons worth 10s. in 1858 household furniture to the value of £1.5s. in 1864 and again in 1865 a copper boiler worth £1. By now the affair was ritual, the goods to be taken in lieu of payment clearly put to one side for a servant to give the bailiff when he called.

Except for the Earlham interlude and a brief spell caring for her brother John's children at Elm Grove she lived all her life in the old family house in Bank Street[7] which had been her parents' home before they moved out to Gastard. She is best remembered for her concern for the welfare of Melksham townspeople, in particular for poor widows and spinsters. To this end she founded in 1784 a clothing charity, the Melksham Almshouse at The City and built and presented to the town the New Hall in the Market Place (now, 1991, the Job Centre) to be used as a reading-room by the general public and for lectures. She engaged vigorously in the temperance movement even though her brother John had resumed the family wine and spirits business which, as we have seen, his father had discontinued[8]. Doubtless to make her point as strongly as she could she established entirely at her own expense a temperance hotel in King Street.

Mary Fowler, later Gurney (1802-1835)

Rachel and her sister Mary were lifelong companions. Both were of a studious disposition, both were steeped in their Quaker faith. Mary's marriage in 1827 to famous Quaker banker and religious thinker and reformer Joseph John Gurney must surely have been a perfect match. A devoted wife and loving step-mother it was while nursing her step-daughter that she contracted the fever which ended her life at the age of 33.

Sir Robert Nicholas Fowler Bt (1828/1891)

Thomas (Rachel's brother) and his wife Lucy having become Londoners, their only son, Robert Nicholas grew up in sur-

*Sir Robert Nicholas Fowler, Lord Mayor of London
for two years in succession*

Gastard House, built by Sir Robert Fowler on the site of Elm Grove, Fowler family home from 1799.

roundings very different from Melksham, where the Quaker broad-brimmed hat, buckled shoes and coat without lapels, particularly on a Fowler, commanded respect, and where the annual visit of the bum-bailiff to distrain goods for unpaid church-rate or tithe had become by now a simple matter of routine. He attended Grove House School, Tottenham, an expensive Quaker-run establishment for the sons of rich Friends. From there, Oxbridge being closed to him as a Quaker, he went on to read Classics and Mathematics at the recently founded (and academically more demanding) University College, London, where he distinguished himself as a winner of prizes.

On going down he was made a partner in his father's bank (Drewett and Fowler, later Prescott and Co). Thereafter he dedicated himself to Tory politics with almost fanatical zeal, making his first task the reorganisation of the party in the City of London.

In 1856 he and his wife Sarah Charlotte, born Fox (1834-1876) of the well-known and influential Quaker family of that name in Falmouth, both birthright Quakers, with their two daughters Lucy and Charlotte, were baptised into the Church of England at Tunbridge Wells. In 1878 he requested Tottenham Monthly Meeting to "disconnect" him and his family. Like many of his generation, Robert had grown away from the Religious Society of Friends, which, for reasons described later, was then in rapid decline. The rest of his public life was spent mainly in service to the Conservative Party. He was successively Member of Parliament for Falmouth and the City of London, was made a baronet and for two years in succession was Lord Mayor of London.

Apart from opposition to traffic in opium and his concern for the welfare of aboriginals, his performance in the House of Commons was distinguished mainly for his loyal support of the party line which, it is said, he would often express with cries redolent of the hunting field. Foreign travel and fox-hunting were his chief delights. In 1862, following the death of his uncle John at Elm Grove the previous year he left London to live there. Thereafter he travelled to China, Japan and India (of which visit he published an account in 1877) and also South Africa and the United States of America. In the meantime he demolished Elm Grove, the old family home, and erected in its place the grandiose Gastard House.

Sir Thomas Fowler Bt (1868-1902)

Sir Robert's only son Thomas moved as far away from the ethos of the Religious Society of Friends as it was possible to go. Arch-Tory, a pillar of the Carlton Club, he fought in South Africa as a captain in the 1st Battalion of the Royal Wilts Imperial Yeomanry Cavalry and was killed in a skirmish at Olivier's

Farm, Moullman's Spruit, Orange Colony, on 20 April 1902, less than a month before the war ended. He was unmarried and the baronetcy expired with him.

Henry Fowler (1823-1880)
John and Rebecca's eldest son, Rachel's nephew, left Melksham for London and prospered as timber merchant, stove manufacturer and tea-dealer. He was joined in London by his younger brother Robert (1825-1888), see below.

John Fowler (1826-1864)
Henry's brother John (Rachel's nephew and John and Rebecca's third son) was the distinguished engineer and inventor. At 17 he was sent to W C Bowly of Cirencester to learn the flour-milling trade, then in 1847 to Quakers Gilkes, Wilson & Leatham at Middlesborough. Later he joined the firm of Fowler & Fry of Bristol, then moved to Ipswich to work with the firm conducted by Quakers Robert Ransome and Charles May (Ransomes & May, later Ransomes & Jefferies). By 1849, when he was still only 23, Ransomes & May were manufacturing his patent horse-drawn draining plough designed in consultation with Bristol agricultural implement maker Quaker Albert Fry. This was the implement used for draining the Hainault marshes. Of the example put on show at the Great Exhibition of 1851 a commentator observed that "but for the American reapers, Mr Fowler's drainage plough would have formed the most remarkable feature in the agricultural department".

Turning to steam, with the cooperation of Ransomes of Ipswich and George and Robert Stephenson of Newcastle, Fowler designed the steam plough which at Chester Show in 1858 won him the prize of £500 offered by the Royal Agricultural Society "for a steam cultivator that shall ... be an economic substitute for the plough and spade".

John Fowler inherited the Fowler business acumen and

founded at Hunslet, Leeds, an engineering firm which employed over 900 workers. His untimely death at the age of 38 resulted from tetanus contracted through injuries received in a fall while fox-hunting at Ackworth in Yorkshire.

The firm, John Fowler and Co (Leeds) Ltd, went from strength to strength. In the words of Michael R Lane in his history of the company[9]:

> At the the turn of the century one would have been hard-pressed to find a single country in the world where Fowler machinery was not at work. The extraordinary contribution made by a small group of largely inter-related Quaker families, of which Fowlers were part, is one of the remarkable phenomena of progress in the nineteenth century.

But by that time the firm had lost all traces of its Quaker ethos. In the words of Isabel A Pelly, great-niece of John Fowler, writing the foreword to Lane's history:

> When wars came we reversed the "swords into ploughshares" tradition and were involved with weapons. In the Boer War we adapted our traction engines to become military transport carriers. In World War I we devised track girdles for gun wheels, and from tracks for gun wheels we experimented in caterpillar tracks for tanks, and in designing the tank itself ...[10]

Robert Fowler (1825-1888)

Besides his partnership in London with his elder brother Henry (see above), Robert went into partnership with his younger brother John in the steam plough manufacturing project and after John's death in 1864 became, in effect, general manager.

John Fowler (1826 - 1864) distinguished agricultural machinery engineer and his wife Elizabeth (1833/81). Elizabeth was the daughter of Joseph Pease, M.P. for Darlington, the first Quaker to enter Parliament.

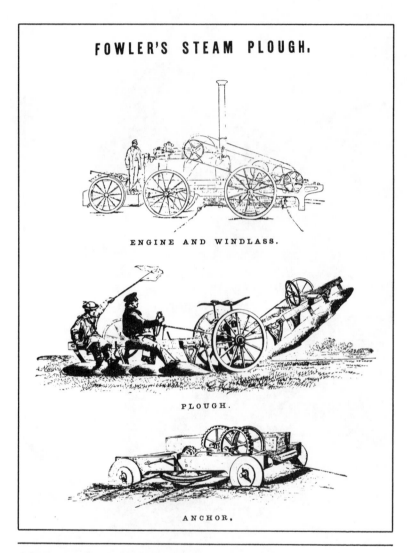

FOWLER'S STEAM PLOUGH.

ENGINE AND WINDLASS.

PLOUGH.

ANCHOR.

John Fowler's prize-winning steam plough as illustrated in Ransome and May's catalogue of about 1860.

In this capacity he became involved with overseas marketing, in particular in Egypt and mainland Europe. In this connexion he was awarded in 1873 a "Knight's Grand Cross of the Highest Order of Franz Josef of Austria". This seems to have been, as awards often are, an inexpensive consolation prize. The Austrian government had made much of their intention to hold in Vienna in 1873 a grand international exhibition to rival the one that had been held by the British in Hyde Park in 1851 and invited the Fowler firm to exhibit. In the event the exhibition flopped, largely through bad organisation compounded by an outbreak of cholera in the city.

William Fowler MP (1828-1905)

William was Rachel's nephew, third son of her brother John, brother of engineer John. William was Melksham-born but pursued his career in London at the Bar and in Parliament. Born in the same year as his cousin Sir Robert they were at University College together, where both read Classics and Mathematics and both did well, William being elected a fellow. Thereafter their paths diverged. Robert, as we have seen, joined the family bank, embraced Conservatism and in due course left the Religious Society of Friends to join the Church of England. William went to the Bar, joined the Liberal Party and stayed a Quaker.

Both William and Robert became Members of Parliament but on opposite sides. William supported the Liberal Party and was member for Cambridge from 1868-74 and from 1880-85. His particular concerns were reform of the law, economics and finance. He married in 1855 Rachel Howard, who died in 1868. In 1871 he married Elizabeth Fox Tuckett of Frenchay, who died the following year. In 1875 he married Rachel, widow of Charles Albert Leatham of Darlington and daughter of Joseph Pease MP.

Jean Elizabeth Fowler (1865-1944)

With the death in action of Sir Thomas in 1902 the Fowler dynasty virtually ceased to exist in Melksham. Sir Thomas had inherited the house at Gastard but he died unmarried and the rest of the family had gone their various ways. His sister Jean, seventh of Sir Robert's ten daughters, was the last member of the family to live there.

Jean was baptised in the Church of England at Corsham and seems to have taken no interest at all in the Religious Society of Friends. In memory of Sir Thomas she gave the Church of St John the Baptist at Gastard, dedicated in 1812.

Writing of his memories of boyhood in Gastard (in *Where the Ladbrook flows*) Bob Hayward remembers her as a "person of most versatile unreliable character", hard on employees yet capable of great compassion, quoting as example her helpfulness to refugees during the first World War. He claims that it was under her management that the family estate consisting of Byde Hill, some twelve to thirteen farms, several surface quarries and two underground quarries declined. It seems that in the 1920s the outlying farms were sold and in further decline Gastard House was let to Lord Methuen and Jean went to live in a bungalow at Goods Hill.

In fairness to Jean it has to be remembered that she had come into the property quite unexpectedly when her brother was killed, and was completely ignorant of estate management. Not all judgments of her character are as harsh as Mr Hayward's. Another local historian John Poulson of Corsham, who learnt something of the circumstances from his parents, is much less scathing. In a letter to me he attributes the break-up of the estate to the incompetence of the bailiff she employed, whose shortcomings will doubtless have been compounded by the depression which followed the First World War and lasted into the early thirties of this century. Mr Poulson tells me that Jean taught wood-carving at the Coffee Tavern (I think this must have been the temperance hotel in King Street, Melksham, which was founded by Rachel Fowler). Mary Bell of Bradford on Avon, great-granddaughter of Sir Robert Fowler, remembers her as kind and generous to her and other children of members of the family who were always made welcome at Gastard House and taken on outings in her Humber car.

Jean Fowler spent the last years of her life at Farnham in Surrey, where she died in 1944. Burial was at Corsham.

NOTES

1. For much of the information about the Fowler family I have drawn on a privately-printed family history lent to me by Mary Bell of Bradford on Avon, great granddaughter of Sir Robert Fowler. This was begun in 1697 and updated by later generations. It was given by Robert Fowler (1755-1825) to his son Thomas (1791-1851) in 1797 for use in the family circle. It was further brought up to date by Lucy Charlotte Fowler (1854-1897). In 1899 Jean (1865-1944) had it printed (by William Lewis and Son, Herald Office, Bath) for distribution to members of the family.

2. WRO 854/50.

3. Melksham town directories for the years 1793-1798.

4. Pseudonym of French writer and satirist François-Marie Arouet (1694-1778) whose first contact with the Religious Society of Friends was probably John Lacey when they were both political prisoners in the Bastille.

5. In the library of Woodbrooke College, Birmingham.

6. An ordained Anglican clergyman could not, in those days, have been also a member of the Religious Society of Friends, so had they married Rachel would have been obliged to resign her membership. Today there are Anglican clergy who are also Quakers, but for early

nineteenth century Quakers and Anglicans that would have been unthinkable.

7. The building stands where Bank Street becomes High Street, facing Lowbourne.

8. When his daughter Mary Jane married Edward Leatham at Melksham Friends Meeting House in October 1851 his occupation was given as wine merchant.

9. *The Story of the Steam Plough Works* (Northgate Publishing Co Ltd).

10. The company closed in 1945. It had been ailing in the 1930s but was kept going during the Second World War under government control as what was in effect a Royal Ordnance Factory for the construction of tanks - Cromwells, Matildas, Centaurs and Comets. At the end of the war, in 1945, it ceased to exist in its own right, though the steam plough works which John Fowler had erected at Hunslet in 1861 was operated until 1974 by Marshall Sons & Co.

9 NORMAN PENNEY, MELKSHAM MISSIONARY

By the late ninetheenth century the Religious Society of Friends was in decline throughout Britain, but nowhere more so than in Wiltshire. Here the decline was more evident because it had started earlier and was therefore more advanced. By 1828 all meeting-houses in the Wiltshire Monthly Meeting had closed except those of Calne and Melksham. In 1858 the meeting-house at Devizes was reopened and meetings resumed. But attendance was poor. In 1874 there were two adult members only. In 1879 it was again closed.

The consciousness of failure gave rise to much soul-searching. The success of the Quaker-inspired Adult School Movement[1] seemed to offer hope. There were Friends with a sense of mission who saw the possibility of building on this success by their presence and personal endeavours. One such was Norman Penney.

Penney was born at Darlington in 1858 and was educated at the Quaker school at Ackworth and also at Minden and Nimes in Provence, where there was an established French Quaker community. He then joined his father's printing firm till the call came to serve the Religious Society of Friends full-time. Under the auspices of the Home Missions Committee, which had been formed in 1882 to help and encourage those who heard the call, he served first at Hawes in his native Yorkshire, then, after a spell in Gloucester, moved on 23 June 1892 to Melksham. He was accompanied by his second wife Mary (born Collinson), whom he had married two years before, their small son and his sister Constance.

SOCIETY OF FRIENDS,
⚜ MELKSHAM. ⚜

On WEDNESDAY, JUNE 26th, 1895,

MEETINGS will be held as under, in the

MEETING HOUSE, KING STREET,

At which Friends from different parts of the country are expected to be present.

At NOON.	At THREE p.m.	At EIGHT p.m.
FOR FRIENDS ONLY.	**A PUBLIC LECTURE**	**A PUBLIC LECTURE**
	Will be given by	Will be given by
SHORT DEVOTIONAL MEETING,	*ELLWOOD BROCKBANK,*	*ELLWOOD BROCKBANK,*
To be followed by a	(Of London), on	(Who has just returned from 12 months' visit to Mount Lebanon), on
CONFERENCE.	"The Attitude of the Society of Friends towards Baptism and the Supper."	"The Home and Foreign Activities of the Society of Friends."
on		
"Our Position in Wiltshire and its Responsibilities."	*CHAIRMAN:*	
	SAMUEL J. ALEXANDER,	*CHAIRMAN:*
With Proposals for a Forward Movement in the County.	(Of Weston-Super-Mare.)	**JOHN MORLAND,** J.P.,
	DISCUSSION INVITED.	(Of Glastonbury.)

The Inhabitants of Melksham and Neighbourhood are warmly invited to be present at the afternoon and evening Meetings. No Collections.

W. JOLLIFFE AND CO., PRINTERS, MELKSHAM.

The Quaker Home Missions Committee was formed in London in 1882 to try to reverse the decline in the Society's membership which was the general throughout the country. In 1892 Norman Penney was despatched to Wiltshire and took up residence at Melksham. Note the Penney-inspired confidence to consider "proposals for a forward movement in the country."

Sunday, Oct. 30. 1892. OPENING OF ADULT SCHOOL.

this long-book
ii forward-to
event com-
menced at
nine am.
15 were pres-
ent, including
visitors, seven
names were
entered on the
Register. We
occupy room
beyond the
shutters, wh.
used to be
called the
Women's 2.
Meeting Ho.
but is now
styled the
Schoolroom.
It will hold
50 a bo with
comfort +
more. if
packed

EXTENSION OF THE
ADULT SCHOOL MOVEMENT
TO MELKSHAM.

In connection with the opening of an

ADULT SCHOOL FOR MEN,

A MEETING to explain the aims and advantages of this movement for the benefit of Working Men

WILL BE HELD IN THE

FRIENDS' MEETING HOUSE,
KING STREET,

ON SATURDAY, OCTOBER 29, 1892,

WHEN

ADDRESSES

WILL BE GIVEN BY

FREDERICK J. WILLIAMS,
(Of the Bristol Schools,)

AND SEVERAL TEACHERS AND

WORKING MEN

MEMBERS OF THE GLOUCESTER SCHOOLS.

DURING THE EVENING THERE WILL BE

VOCAL AND CONCERTINA SOLOS,

And an Exhibition of Photographs and other objects of Adult School Interest.

THE CHAIR WILL BE TAKEN AT 7.30 PROMPT, BY

NORMAN PENNEY.

ALL ARE WARMLY INVITED TO ATTEND.

JOLLIFFE AND CO., PRINTERS, MELKSHAM.

He threw himself into the work with enthusiasm. His diary, preserved at Friends House, London, tells of patient efforts to get meetings going again. Long-closed meeting-houses were reopened and the public invited to take part in specially-called prayer-meetings or to hear addresses by visiting Quaker speakers. It was a brave try; but the missionary approach was alien to Quaker ways and tradition and in the end failed.

He fared somewhat better with his efforts on behalf of the Adult School Movement. An inaugural meeting was held at the Melksham meeting-house in October 1892. He recorded in his diary that fifteen persons came and seven names were entered in the register. He pursued the project in other towns in disused meeting-houses which had once known substantial Quaker congregations, offering a wide range of improving talks and lantern-lectures. Where appropriate he would appear in costume; in those pre-cinema and pre-television days that will doubtless have been a revelation to an unsophisticated audience. He reported attendances of over forty.[2]

As might be expected, he was called upon to take his share in conducting the affairs of the North Somerset and Wiltshire Monthly Meeting, as it had now become, and among other things was its registering officer for marriages, an important appointment given the wide latitude allowed to Friends in the arrangement and conduct of their marriages.[3] He also made himself active in local government and in 1895 was elected to the Melksham Urban District Council. In the same year he was co-founder with Charles Maggs, chairman of the UDC and a prominent local Methodist, of the Wiltshire Parochial Electors' Association.

A determinedly optimistic passage in the Annual Report for 1896 of London Yearly Meeting claims that at Melksham "good meetings are held in the old building and the general work is well maintained". But in truth, so far as the revival of Quakerism in Wiltshire was concerned, Penney was swimming

Norman Penney of the Quaker Home Missions Committee. He is wearing the costume which he described as that of a Damascus merchant and used by way of illustration for his Adult School lectures.

against the tide. No meetings were re-started and the two existing ones, Calne and Melksham, declined still further to the point where it was no longer considered necessary to have a clerk for each, one sufficing for both. A few years later the Calne meeting-house closed its doors for good.[4]

The Melksham Adult School continued while Penney was in Melksham. But by the 1890s, thanks to the Education Acts, any young adults who were inclined to read the Bible or anything else had been equipped to do so. Although the movement continued to flourish for a few years longer elsewhere in the country in Wiltshire it does not seem to have long survived Norman Penney's departure in 1898. In that year the Home Missions Committee transferred him to Tottenham, but, his missionary zeal now evidently diminished, in 1901 we find London Yearly Meeting reporting that he "is largely engaged on library work ... but continues his work at Tottenham so far as circumstances permit". The following year it is reported that he has given up mission work to become the first librarian at Devonshire House, in London, the then central offices of the society.

Penney had at last found his proper niche. From now on his consuming interest was the society's history. He was joint founder of the Friends Historical Society and for thirty years was editor of that society's journal. In 1924 he was made an honorary Doctor of Letters by Haverford College, the American Quaker university. He died in 1933 aged 75.

Opposite and overleaf: *Lectures and addresses*

LIST OF

LECTURES & ADDRESSES

GIVEN BY

NORMAN PENNEY,

BETH-SEPHER,

MELKSHAM (WILTS).

Exhibitions of Eastern Life.

With Costumes, Curiosities,
      Working Models, Pictures,
            Diagrams, a Tent, etc.,

Obtained during a Visit to Palestine in 1888,

and all explanatory of the Bible.

———

These exhibitions, which can be extended over more than
one evening if desired, have been given in various parts of the
country, and have proved amusing and instructive.

By special arrangement.

Short Sketches of Strange Scenes.

ILLUSTRATED.

The Mirror of Scripture Lands.
Egypt by Land and Water.
The Bedaween of the Bible.
A Pisgah View of Canaan.
Jerusalem in Honour and Dishonour.
Up the Country on Horse, Mule, and Camel.
Life at the Well's Mouth.
The Peasantry of Palestine.
Proverbs and Compliments.
Among the Samaritans.
A City for Four Thousand Years.
Exploration in Palestine.
A Day in a Lebanon Mission School.
Eastern Dress and its Teaching.
Births, Deaths, and Marriages.
On the Track of Paul's Voyage to Rome.
"Stamboul by the Sea."
Sixteen Hundred Miles in the Orient Express.

Biblical.

The Bible, written, copied, translated, printed, read, distributed, preached, sold, smuggled, hidden, chained, baked, burnt, and buried. *With diagrams.*

The Pilgrim's Progress, Part one. *Twenty diagrams.*

The Pilgrim's Progress, Part two. *Twelve diagrams.*

The Dividing of Time: Old Testament Chronology taught by means of a *Plank and Pegs.*

"From Adam until Moses." The descent of Knowledge through 25 centuries, *illustrated by a large, specially-prepared Sheet and Wooden Bridge.*

Bible Making in Bible Times. An account of the gradual collection of the Biblical records.

The Wanderings of the Sacred Chest. *With model, diagram, and map.*

BIBLICAL (continued).

The Seven Words from the Cross.

Our Lord's Conversations with His Apostles. *Parts to be taken by thirteen persons.*

"The Life of David, as reflected in his Psalms." With an original scheme of the Davidic portions of the Psalter.

The Songs of the Temple Pilgrims. Psalms 120-134. *Illustrated by maps and pictures.*

Lessons, Spiritual and Moral from the Book of Tobit.

Pedigrees, Outward and Spiritual.

Characteristics of the Four Gospels.

"Ye are the Light of the World." *Object Lesson with the aid of various kinds and colours of candles.*

BIBLICAL (continued).

Texts illustrated by Travels. *With many models.*

Heavenly Arithmetic.

Notes from my Bible margins. With hints on quoting from Scripture, and some advice to Bible students.

The Peerage of Heaven.

The Position of Woman in the Christian Polity, Contrasted with her condition under other religious systems.

Old and New Testament Angelophanies.

Some Thoughts on the Resurrection Morning.

"Measure for Measure": or, The Bible Nemesis.

Lessons from Trades: Printing

6

BIBLICAL (continued).

Our Lord "Shadowed" by Scribes and Pharisees.

Links in the Chain of Old Testament Prophecy concerning the Christ.

Bible Prisons and their Occupants.

Life Sketches :
Abraham. *Illustrated by maps.*
Joshua.   „   „
Samuel.   „   „
Saul.   „   „
David.   „   „
Paul.   „   „

Sayings of Christ unrecorded in the Gospels.

Joseph as a Type of Christ.

Child Views of Heaven.

Man in his Relation to the Rest of the Creation.

7

Band of Hope.

The Picture Gallery of Bacchus.
With some reproductions of Public House Signs.

The Value of Water in Hot Countries.
With models.

Seven Kings and their Subjects.

And various other short Temperance Addresses.

Foreign Missions.

History of the Friends' Syrian Mission.

Visits to Continental and Eastern Meetings of Friends.

The Sufferings of Children in Heathen Lands.
Six diagrams.

8

Social Purity.

"Call a Spade a Spade," and other plain talks.

Ramblings in One Hundred Hymns.

Billy Bray's Life Lessons.

Sammy Hick's Stimulating History.

The Origin and Meaning of Common Sayings.

The Story of Bradshaw's Guide.

Prison Scribbles and their Lessons.

Experiences of Work in connection with Adult Schools.

SOCIETY OF FRIENDS.

The Inhabitants of
BRADFORD-ON-AVON
are cordially invited to attend
A MEETING
FOR DIVINE WORSHIP
To be held in the
FRIENDS MEETING HOUSE,
(Technical School Laboratory)
NEAR ST. MARGARET STREET, ON
TUESDAY, SEP. 25th, 1894,
at Eight p.m.

Several Ministers and other Friends intend to
be present at the Meeting.
NO COLLECTION.

C. RAWLING, PRINTER, BRADFORD-ON-AVON.

*Norman Penney strove to reactivate closed Quaker Meetings but met
with little success.*

NOTES

1. The origins of the Adult School Movement go back to 1810 in Bristol, when Quaker Dr. Thomas Pole (1753-1829) a friend and helper of Quaker Joseph Lancaster set to work to teach illiterates to read. The school was held in the Quaker meeting-house known as Friars and rapidly grew to over 1500 men and women. Scope was limited; students had to leave as soon as they could read the Bible.

Later on, in 1847, the Friends' First-day School Association under Joseph Storrs Fry of Bristol boosted the movement by widening its scope to include, besides early morning classes for study and discussion, meetings for family worship. Members might be of any denomination or none. The organisation took on the character of a high-minded working-people's club. Long-empty meeting-houses were brought back into full use. The movement not only satisfied the needs of the day — by the end of the century there were 50,000 members throughout the country — but also took the Friends out of themselves to close association, on equal terms before God, with a class to which, to their loss, they had long since ceased to belong.

2. *The Friend* (the weekly journal of the Religious Society of Friends) reported on 21 October 1892 that Penney had given an address on The Voyage of Life with magic lantern views in a large hall well filled by an audience, many of whom "usually stroll the streets on a Sunday evening". On 14 November a large audience attended his Eastern Entertainment and an exhibition in the YMCA rooms.

3. Quaker marriages. From the very beginning in mid-seventeenth century Quakers refused to acknowledge the authority of the Church of England and conducted their marriages in their own meeting places under common law. Though the validity of these marriages was challenged from time to time (c/f the need to raise funds to cover legal costs in 1744) they were upheld by the law, which, in due course, accorded the society the right to conduct marriages much as they pleased subject only to subsequent registration. This privilege continues to this day.

4. The building (in Wood Street) is now a betting-shop.

10 OCCUPATIONS

In the earliest days in Melksham, Friends Meeting comprised artisans, tradesmen, yeoman farmers and small business people. Two centuries later there were Melksham Quakers who had not only entered the upper middle class but also, as we have seen, walked at national level the corridors of power, with bankers calling the financial tune and a member on each side of the House of Commons.

Of the earliest Melksham Quakers whose occupations are revealed in the records, sixteen were engaged in the major local industries of clothing and brewing; there were seven maltsters, three clothiers, three weavers, one clothworker, one feltmaker and one woolcomber. Three members were a family of yeoman farmers named Pinnock, two were domestic servants (husband and wife employed by William Smith, later of Bromham House), one was a grocer, one a joiner, one a tallow-chandler and one a tailor.

From 1730 some occupations no longer appear:

woolcomber

tallowchandler

and between then and 1770 new ones are found:

baker

mercer

apothecary

draper

After 1770 there are no more weavers but between then and 1800 we find new trades and callings:

dealer in spirits

miller

mealman
physician
banker
From 1800 more new ones:
brush manufacturer
builder and plasterer
ironmonger
warehouseman
tea dealer
wine merchant

Gradually occupations had changed to reflect change outside the Society of Friends as well as within it. As time went on there were, in Melksham, fewer clothiers and maltsters; instead there were bankers, tea dealers, wine merchants and small manufacturers.

Farming continued without a break and there were always yeomen and husbandmen who combined their agricultural activities with a corresponding commercial venture such as malting, cheese-making or cloth manufacture. John Rutty, Senior, was farmer, clothier, cheesemonger, maltster and grocer. William Smith, who farmed at Whitley, was also clothier and maltster; from him, in 1704 parson Bohun Fox seized 9 bushels of malt and clothing material worth £7.16s. and in subsequent years hay, barley, wheat, bread and malt. In 1710 John Somner of Seend Row had hay and malt taken. Later on we find that often the farm is ancillary to the main occupation and that even the doctor ran one; in 1801 the vicar took from William Tully MD hay worth £33.10s.

A survey of occupations of Melksham Quakers during the first half of the present century up to its closure would have revealed almost all to be in the white-collar category, of whom a high proportion engaged in such fields as government, teaching, accountancy, social work and medicine.

11   THE END OF AN ERA

By the end of the nineteenth century the Melksham Quaker Meeting, though in decline, was still viable; we can form an impression of it from Henry Baron Smith's recollections in 1902 (*see* Appendix E). There was, however, little, if any, new blood. Such members as remained were aged; the rest were dead, disowned, deserters to another persuasion or, like the Fowler family, gone off to fresh fields of endeavour elsewhere.

The decline in numbers was general throughout Britain. In the early days the Quakers believed they had a message for the world. In the seventeenth century they had been the largest body of dissenters in the country, numbering some 50,000, more than one in every hundred of the population. In 1950, the year that Melksham Meeting closed, British membership was about 20,000 or one in every 2,500.

Paradoxically, as numbers went down, standing and influence on the nation's political, social and economic life had grown. A network of Quaker bankers, industrialists and traders wielded considerable influence in the business world and out of this grew political power. In the nineteenth century, for the first time, a Quaker was elected to Parliament (Joseph Pease, member for South Durham 1832-1842) and a Quaker, John Bright, held office as a leading member of Gladstone's government from 1868.

But decline in Wiltshire led to collapse and near-oblivion. It began early on, in part at least stemming from the 1670s with the activities of John Wilkinson and John Story, disaffected members from Westmorland. Their activities were disruptive elsewhere but nowhere more damaging than in Wiltshire.

George Fox recorded in his journal:

> 1673 ... I came into Wiltshire where we had many
> precious meetings, though some opposition by one
> Nathaniel Coleman against the women's meetings
> at Slaughterford. But as he went out of the house
> in a rage and passion, he saw the angel of the Lord
> stand ready with his drawn sword to cut him off.
> And he said he was a dead man and desired me
> to pray for him, and said he was a dead man and
> desired me to forgive him. And I told him if he felt
> forgiveness from the Lord whom he had opposed,
> I would freely forgive him.

Coleman's repentance proved short-lived. In 1680 we find
him named again as a leading troublemaker[1].

For a while the damage did not show. The Toleration Act
of 1689 breached the dam of frustration generated by the years
of repression and persecution to produce a spate of activity.
Between 1689 and 1735 new meeting-houses were built or old
ones refurbished at Bishop's Cannings (1689), Calne (1697),
Hullavington (1697), Melksham (1699), Devizes (1702), Purton
(1705), Urchfont (1707), (Lavington 1707 - rebuilt 1714), Corsham (1710), Bromham (1712), Sarum (1712), Bradford on Avon
(1718), Marlborough (1721) and Chippenham (by 1734). Besides these, in the same period, some 47 private dwellings were
registered as Quaker places of worship. The expansion proved
illusory. By the end of the eighteenth century the only meeting-
houses still open were those at Devizes, Hullavington and
Melksham and total membership in the county was down to
150. Long before the end of the next century Wiltshire Monthly
Meeting ceased to exist in its own right, being joined in 1876
to North Somerset Monthly Meeting.

All over Britain the end of persecution heralded an era in

which Quakers moved from radical defiance to institutional conventionality and became acceptable to the authorities and the community at large. In Wiltshire, as elsewhere, they were now seen as idosyncratic but respectable and trustworthy. Many became well-to-do. From being a vociferous movement of seekers after religious truth, the Society had become a largely conventional community with standard materialist values. Quaker John Hackett of Frome, Somerset, was among those who deplored it. In a letter dated 15 July 1732 to his friend Thomas Bennet, (the Quaker schoolmaster at Corsham) he lamented the prevailing spiritual weakness and serving of Mammon, losses by death and a dearth of new members[3]. But the decline went on.

The family solidarity which had been such a source of strength in the times of tribulation (and in some cases an aid to the amassing of considerable private fortunes) contained the seeds of its own destruction. By the nineteenth century the family network created by the rule against "marrying out" was formidable. To William Cobbett Wiltshire Quakers were members of a "villanous tribe", and tribal they certainly were, though the qualifying adjective was too sweeping and harsh. But the "marrying out" rule cost the Society many valuable members. When it was at last abolished in 1859 it was noted that under it some 5,000 had been expelled in the preceding 50 years.

In Wiltshire factors peculiar to the county were at work. The clothing industry by which many Quakers had prospered was in decline. Younger members of the leading Quaker families were educated, ambitious and restless. Bristol was a magnet, so was London and so was Pennsylvania in the New World. As Quakers, many were more strongly attached to their Quaker community than to the locality in which they had grown up and were not reluctant to go elsewhere in search of employment or apprenticeships, invariably to Quaker employers. We have seen, for example, how some members of the Fowler family moved away within the Quaker network; and how others, having acquired the ways of the local gentry, felt themselves oppressed by Quaker rules and peculiarities, and to some extent segregated by them, left the society for the relative freedom of the Church of England.

Bright young men from well-to-do families, as Quakers barred from the then Anglican-controlled Oxbridge colleges, left for education or professional training elsewhere, frequently in Dublin, Edinburgh or Holland. Others, when business was bad, left for Bristol or London. At all times, permitted only to marry a fellow-member if they wished to remain in the society, the young were apt to marry members they had met at London or Bristol annual general meetings or other Quaker regional gatherings.

In the nature of things there are, in all communities, the leaders and the led; Quakerism, by its very nature, called for strong and active leadership and in the early days, at least, fairly long purses. As the minute-books show, it was customary to hold Quaker business meetings in the houses of members. These will almost certainly have been the large houses of the more prosperous ones, which those lower down on the social scale may well have been too diffident to enter. And when leaders moved away some will have found the burden of what was expected of them, in a church which had no paid ministry, greater than they were willing or able to bear and found less demanding denominations attractive. Family names which formerly appeared frequently in Quaker records later appear in Methodist[4] ones; in June 1804 Samuel Rutty and Abraham Shewring are named in Methodist registration certificates. Others found the Moravian sect attractive[5].

It is significant, in this connexion, that shortly after the Meeting at Lavington was closed in 1795, the meeting-house was sold to the Congregationalists; and the one at Chippenham, after being used for a while as a "schoolroom for the education of female adults of any religious persuasion residing in Chippenham or its vicinity", was sold to Primitive Methodists.

A great weakness in the Society everywhere in Britain was the automatic enrolment of children. From 1737 children of members automatically became themselves members from birth. Many of these "birthright" Friends, Quakers in name only and part of the Quaker community willy-nilly, contributed nothing to its spiritual life, and stayed members more from habit than conviction. Lowered standards could justify Karl Marx's fulminations against nineteenth century Quaker capitalists, so different were they from the seventeeth century one, John Bellers, Marx's exemplar of industrial beneficence.

The Friends of the nineteenth century were a world away from the travelling preacher in leather breeches who had so stirred hearts and minds in the early days. Few wished to join. Gentle Charles Lamb's lovingly sympathetic description of Quaker meeting for worship[6] and his confession that although he loved Quaker ways and Quaker worship and venerated Quaker principles he could not like the Quakers "to live with them"[7] speaks volumes. By 1864 membership nationwide was down to 13,735.

But Quakerism did survive, and did so because in some hearts the old fire still burned brightly. Individual Friends were pioneers of reform, both inside and outside the Society of Friends, not least among them, as noted above, Rachel Fowler's in-laws, the Gurneys, the Frys and the Buxtons. Joseph John Gurney, Mary Fowler's husband, was, in fact, the earliest and most vigorous advocate of the kind of reform which turned the society upside down in the second half of the nineteenth century. Reform slowly brought new life. Not without strong opposition peculiarities of speech and garb were abandoned, marriage rules relaxed, attendance at a place of worship other than the Friends meeting-house was no longer forbidden, gravestones were permitted for such as desired them and missionary work was no longer discouraged.

But in Wiltshire it was all too late. Nothing could save Melksham, Meeting, not even the efforts of the Home Missions Committee and tireless Norman Penney. After 1914 one or two members met for worship only; no longer were there meetings for Quaker business because there was no business to transact. In 1918 Melksham Meeting was merged with Bath Meeting. In 1950 Melksham Friends meeting-house closed its doors for the last time.

NOTES

1. The Separatists challenged the leadership's policy, in particular the status of women as equals with men in the conduct of the Society's affairs. They objected to the procedure by which couples intending to marry had to lay their intentions before the women as well as the men's Monthly Meeting. Their attitude in this respect reflected the popular attitudes and prejudices of the day.. We may recall Dr Samuel Johnson's comment to Boswell when he said that he had been to a Quaker Meeting and that one of the speakers was a woman:

> Sir, a woman's preaching is like a dog's walking on his hind legs. It is not done well; but you are surprised to see it done at all.

The Separatists sought to take control by setting up "Separate" Meetings and even by disrupting existing ones. They were most active in Wiltshire and neighbouring Berkshire and, though by about 1716 the movement had fizzled out, damage had been done, in Wiltshire especially.

In the past, official attempts at suppression had always led to a closing of ranks. Not so the Second Conventicle Act of 1670; this statute imposed on Quakers fresh penalties even harsher than before.

These included crippling fines for preaching at a Quaker meeting and on the owner of the premises where the meeting was held. Though most meetings continued to meet openly, defying an unjust law, a few others, fearful of the consequences of so doing, shunned private houses and met unobtrusively in secluded places in the open air. It was the beginning of schism; the clandestine meetings came under heavy censure from visiting ministers and other leaders. Disagreement led to alienation. Having themselves been challenged they in turn challenged the policies of the parent body.

Wilkinson and Story and their adherents wreaked havoc in Wiltshire. The minutes of the Quarterly Meeting held at Devizes in April 1678 record major disruption:-

> Upon some occasion of disturbance given ... in a very unfriendly manner, they katched up and Carried away ye Quarterly booke from ye Meeting to an Inn and would not send it again or Returne themselves although some Friends went to them from ye Meeting and Earnestly desired it of them.

A statement at Quarterly Meeting held at Charlcutt 4.8.1680 (4 October 1680) signed by 36 Friends records in part:-

> Whereas ye people of the Lord in the County of Wilts in particular ye Quarterly Meeting thereof have been beyond Expression Exercised with a sad And Lammentable sisme and Divission; ffirst fomented and stewed up by: John Story and John Wilkinson of Westmoreland. And afterwards carried on by severall in this County: the chief whereof was Arthur Eastmead, Nathaniel Coleman: John Jennings and John Matravers: whoe appeared for many Moneths with all their Endeavours to Scatter Devide: and to lay weast our Quarterly Monthly and Women's Meetings which they were in times past very zealous for: which Meetings was Constituted and set up by ye moveings and guidings of ye most high God ... And now for as much as we did labor through great Sufferrings heavy burthens and unexpressible Sorrow

for a long time with these men and those Joyned with them whilst with us in our Quarterly Meeting and Monethly Meetings Being often bowed before ye Lord for them: With Endeavors to reclaim them yet after all They in a very unchristian manner: Sepparated from us takeing away at one of our Quarterly meetings our Quarterly book and Retaines it with our publick Stock untill this day.

The loss of some early Wiltshire minute-books and records is probably attributable to the activities of the Separatists.

2. *Wiltshire Meeting House Certificates 1689-1852,* John Chandler editor. (Wiltshire Record Society.

3. WRO 1699/115.

4. Methodism flourished in the Wiltshire/Somerset area. Itinerant speakers, including John Wesley himself, frequently visited Wiltshire towns on preaching missions.

5.. The Moravian Brethren had some beliefs in common with the Quakers. They rejected formal creeds and in general stood for a simple and unworldly form of Christianity. They did, however, retain the offices of bishop, presbyter and deacon and it may well have been this form of leadership which appealed to rank and file members.

6. *Essays of Elia* (1821)..

7. *Essays of Elia* (1823).

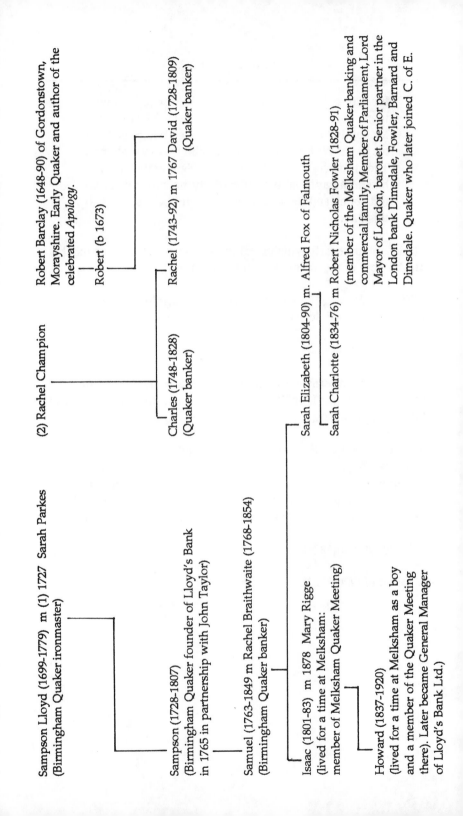

Robert Barclay (1648-90) of Gordonstown, Morayshire. Early Quaker and author of the celebrated *Apology*.

Robert (b 1673)

Rachel (1743-92) m 1767 David (1728-1809) (Quaker banker)

(2) Rachel Champion

Charles (1748-1828) (Quaker banker)

Sampson Lloyd (1699-1779) m (1) 1727 Sarah Parkes (Birmingham Quaker ironmaster)

Sampson (1728-1807) (Birmingham Quaker founder of Lloyd's Bank in 1765 in partnership with John Taylor)

Samuel (1763-1849 m Rachel Braithwaite (1768-1854) (Birmingham Quaker banker)

Sarah Elizabeth (1804-90) m. Alfred Fox of Falmouth

Sarah Charlotte (1834-76) m Robert Nicholas Fowler (1828-91) (member of the Melksham Quaker banking and commercial family, Member of Parliament, Lord Mayor of London, baronet. Senior partner in the London bank Dimsdale, Fowler, Barnard and Dimsdale. Quaker who later joined C. of E.

Isaac (1801-83) m 1878 Mary Rigge (lived for a time at Melksham: member of Melksham Quaker Meeting)

Howard (1837-1920) (lived for a time at Melksham as a boy and a member of the Quaker Meeting there). Later became General Manager of Lloyd's Bank Ltd.)

APPENDIX A

THE MELKSHAM QUAKER BANKERS

The Fowlers of Melksham, substantial bankers themselves, were linked by marriage to Barclays, Frys, Gurneys and Lloyds, the leading bankers of the day.

Mary Fowler (1802/35) married banker Joseph John Gurney, whose sister Elizabeth (the prison reformer) was married to banker Joseph Fry of Norwich.

Henry Fowler (1823-80) was married to Anne Ford Barclay (1822-1913).

Robert Nicholas Fowler (1828-91) married Sarah Charlotte Fox (1834-76) great-granddaughter of Sampson Lloyd (1728-1807) with whom Lloyd's bank started in 1765.

Howard Lloyd (1837-1920)

The man who did more than anyone else to shape the Lloyds Bank we know today, Howard Lloyd (1837-1920), was, as a very small boy, a member of Melksham Meeting after his parents, Isaac (1801-1883) and Mary moved to King Street, Melksham, from Poole in 1841, when Isaac seems to have retired. Although the Quaker register recording the family's transfer of membership gives his occupation as "accountant", Pigott's Directory for 1843 accords him the status of "gentleman". Up to then he had been in the banking business, first with Christy Lloyd and Co (otherwise the Stockport and East Cheshire Bank), then with the Wilts and Dorset Bank.

To judge by Humphrey Lloyd's family history *The Quaker Lloyds in the Industrial Revolution* Isaac seems to have been a rather unsettled person, not very good at anything, particu-

Opposite: *The Quaker banking families networks Barclays, Fowler and Lloyds (the genealogical table on pages 78/79 illustrates Melksham Quaker links by marriage with bankers Fry and Gurney).*

larly bad at handling money and seemingly needing financial help from his parents from time to time. Humphrey Lloyd notes that Isaac's father Samuel created trusts in his will for Isaac and his family, something which he did not think necessary for his other sons.

Isaac and family left Melksham in 1843, the Quaker register recording that they had transferred to the North Somerset Monthly Meeting.

Unlike his father, who clearly had no enthusiasm at all for banking, Howard (1837-1920) was outstandingly successful at it. In 1865 he was appointed general manager of Lloyd's Banking Co Ltd, the joint-stock company newly formed to succeed the century-old Quaker banking partnership founded by Sampson Lloyd. By the time he retired 37 years later the bank was of national and international renown.

The National Westminster Bank

This bank can also trace its origins to the Fowlers of Melksham. The London banking partnership, Drewett & Fowler, was linked with the Melksham banking operation of which Thomas Fowler (1791-1851) became a partner in 1823. In 1868 Drewett & Fowler became Dimsdale, Fowler, Barnard & Dimsdale, at 50 Cornhill. (Sir) Robert Nicholas Fowler succeeded his father as partner there. In due course the bank was incorporated as a joint-stock company. The National Westminster Bank is its descendant.

APPENDIX B

QUAKER MEETING HOUSES AND BURIAL GROUNDS IN WILTSHIRE SINCE THE BEGINNING OF THE MOVEMENT

Alderbury. Burial ground.

1725. Burial ground existed. "Writings" (deeds and documents) referred to in Quarterly Meeting minutes 5 July 1725 (WRO 1699/40).

Bishops Cannings. Meeting-house and burial ground.

1689. At "Wicke" in Bishops Cannings, registration of a house newly-erected in a close called the Quakers burying place. (Item 23 on page 3 of Wiltshire Meeting House Certificates 1689-1852, published by Wiltshire Record Society).

Bradford on Avon. Meeting-houses and burial grounds.

1660. Friends were meeting for worship at Cumberwell.

1661. First recorded burial at Cumberwell.

1676. Had their own meeting-house at Cumberwell as well as a burial ground.

1690. Cumberwell meeting-house registered as a Quaker place of worship.

1718. New meeting-house built in town centre, with burial ground attached

1798. Only one member left and shortly after meeting closed.

1803 Last interment (Ann Eyles of Bradford, wife of James, aged 81).

1806 Building put to use as a school for poor children, later on as a British School.

1813 Former meeting-house and burial ground at Cumberwell sold.

1902. Meeting-house in town centre sold.

1971. Meeting-house established at 1 Whitehead's Lane and regular meetings resumed.

Brinkworth. *See* Lea and Brinkworth.

Bromham. Meeting-house and burial ground.

1682. Assignment of property at Westbrook by Benjamin Shell of Rowde and John Hickman of Bromham to William Smith, Daniel Bayly and others.

1690 Meeting-house registered as a Quaker place of worship.

1712 New meeting-house built. Undated document of about 1800 (WRO 854/39) describes "Bromham meeting-house and burial ground situate in a Common near Bromham in the parish of Bromham in the county of Wilts including the spaces occupied by the meeting-house, tenements etc contains 31 and three quarters poles and is bounded...on the south... by Bromham

Common."
There is a sketch-plan at WRO 1699/104.

1825. Last burial

1863. Meeting-house demolished.

1926. Burial ground sold.

Calne. Meeting-house and burial ground.

1660. Plot of ground at Wood Street acquired by Israel Noyes from Mary Pilgrim.

1672. Plot of ground at Wood Street given to Society of Friends by Israel Noyes of Calne.

1690. Meeting-house registered as a Quaker place of worship.

1695. Quakers plan to build a new meeting-house. (Wilts Quarterly Meeting minute of 8 July 1695 - WRO 1699/38). Money was subscribed and building presumably went ahead.

1840. Meeting-house rebuilt.

1874. Only one member left. Meeting closed.

1962. Meeting-house and burial ground sold. (Premises are now a betting-shop).

Charlcutt. Meeting-house and burial ground.

1690. "The house of the widow Joan Hall at Charlcote in Bremhill" registered as a Quaker place of worship.

1693. Cottage leased to Friends evidently for use as a meeting-house.

1719. Meeting-house and burial ground existed. (Deeds and documents referred to in Quarterly Meeting minute of 21 September 1719).

1808. Premises fell into the possession of the Lord of the Manor on the death of the last surviving trustee, William Storrs Fry, who died 15 October 1808.

Chippenham. Meeting-house and burial ground.

1669. Meeting-house created in Chippenham High Street (later renamed The Causeway).

1690. Meeting-house registered as a Quaker place of worship.

1700. Burial ground "on the Calne road, near the town" acquired.

1734. Meeting-house rebuilt. (Wiltshire Quarterly Meeting minute of 8 April 1734 - WRO 1699/40).

1809. Meeting-house closed.

1822. Meeting-house leased "as a schoolroom for the education of female adults of any religious persuasion residing at Chippenham or its vicinity".

1834. Meeting-house sold to Primitive Methodists. (Now forms part of the Primitive Methodist chapel in The Causeway).

1927 Burial ground sold.

Corsham/Pickwick. Meeting-houses and burial grounds.

1659. Burial ground acquired at Pickwick by copyhold from the Manor of Corsham. This records that "Thomas Davis junior surrenders according to the custom of the manor all that his plot or parcell of ground containing by estimation one farthingale more or less situate in the tything of Pickwick. To the use and behoof of the said Thomas Davis, James Matravers and others to employ the same as a burial ground for the people in scorn called Quakers".
The picturesque bulding known as "Monks" (which has a burial ground attached) is believed to have been erected as a Quaker meeting-house about then.

1690. Meeting-house registered as a Quaker place of worship.

1709. New meeting-house at Corsham.

1774. The offer of Charles Arnold of Corsham to erect a new meeting-house on land adjoining the burial ground at Pickwick in exchange for the old meeting-house at Corsham is accepted (Minute of Quarterly Meeting held March 1774).

1815. Pickwick meeting-house closed.

1879. Meeting-house and burial ground rented to Gabriel

Goldney, owner of adjoining property, who lends it to a working men's club of 42 members. "A vault bore the name Dickinson of Monks ... one stone bears the date 1641". (Report of visit of inspection at WRO 8854/44).

1885. Report by Quaker William Pumphrey (WRO 8854/44):- "The graveyard is very uneven with vaults broken in and stones lying about...the whole place having a very deserted appearance...no indication that it belongs to Friends".

1828. Last burial.

1915. Burial ground sold to Arthur F Bruton. Later on the meeting-house was sold. It is now a Freemasons' lodge.

Devizes. Meeting-house and burial ground.

1647. John Pearce acquired "two tenements on the Greene" which later became Devizes Friends meeting-house.

1665. Burial ground of half an acre acquired (WRO 2269/49).

1690. "The house called the meeting-house on the Greene" was registered as a Quaker place of worship.

1702. New meeting-house built in town centre (High Street) and old one sold (Wiltshire Quarterly Meeting July 1702 and April 1703 - WRO 1699/38).

1817. Last interment.

1826. Meeting-house closed and building let to the Literary and Scientific Institution.

1840, Sold to George Simpson "by direction of Quarterly Meeting". (WRO854/39).

1858. Building taken back into Friends' ownership.

1878. Meetings for worship discontinued.

1890. Building leased to YMCA for 21 years.

1905. Burial ground sold.

1925. Building let to a printer.

1929. Building sold (for £600) to Robert Barron Sloper of Devizes.

1991. New property acquired at Sussex Wharf, Devizes.

Fovant. Burial ground

1705. Given by will of Widow Dunn 27 March 1705. (WRO 854/34). Nothing further known.

Goatacre. Burial ground. Grid reference 020769

1678. Acquired.

1744. Burial of John Beckett. (Stone noted during a property inspection in 1925 - WRO 1699/108).

1785. Last interment.

1867. Leased to Primitive Methodists for 60 years to build a chapel.

1879. "A vigorous though poor congregation [of Primitive Methodists] here. We gave permission for the burial of Anthony Smith and Farmer Wade who have been long connected with the place and wish to be buried there" (Report of visiting committee - WRO 854/44)

1888. Visiting committee noted unauthorised burial of one Blackham.

1909. Chapel removed.

1986. Sold.

Heddington. Burial ground. ST 992662.

1739. Acquired

1925. Tour of inspection (WRO 1699/108) noted "quite a small patch away from everywhere enclosed with hedges such as they are and no stones to show that it had ever been a grave-yard".

1930. Sold.

Hullavington. Meeting-house and burial ground. Grid reference 898817

1654. "Messuage, tenement and new-built house with court, backside and garden" acquired.

1697. Deed (lease for 2000 years) showed meeting-house and burial ground existed but no record of meeting-house registration. The meeting-house stood on the north side of Corner Lane, with a yard to the east and burial ground to the west, with stable and offices at the south-west corner of the burial ground (WRO 1699/104).

1817. Meeting-house closed.

1832. Last burial.

1867. Building in use as a British School.

1879. In use as a Primitive Methodist Chapel and School.

1895. Norman Penney (Quakeriana page 105 Vol II No 7 - library of Friends House, London) wrote: "A meeting-house once stood on the ground but it has been partially pulled down and partly built into a Primitive Methodist chapel. It is curious to see the woodwork of the ministers' gallery and a side seat or two at one end of the house dissolving into the more modern furniture of a chapel".

1902. Meeting-house and burial ground sold for £60, proceeds used to repair meeting-house at Devizes.

Lavington. Meeting-house and burial ground. SU 020545.

1690. "The house of Isaac Selfe" was registered as a Quaker place of worship.

1713. Meeting-house and burial ground existed.

1716. New meeting-house built (High Street).

1795. Meeting given up.

1800. Meeting-house and burial ground sold (to Congregation-alists).

Lea and Brinkworth. Meeting-houses and burial ground.

1690. Meeting-houses registered at both Lea and Brinkworth.

1691. Burial ground at Lea "acquired by deed of gift from Anthony and Ann Sharp of Dublin". Located on Malmesbury-Brinkworth road.

1771. Last interment. Gravestones of the Young family existed dated 1729 to 1771.

1925. Four tombstones with the name Young inscribed still in place
(property inspection in 1925 - WRO 1699/108).

1935. Burial ground sold to Alfred Slade of Lea. Meeting-house had passed out of ownership long before.

Luckington. Burial ground.

1735. No purpose-built meeting-house but the houses of Mary Burnley and Sarah Burnley registered as Quaker places of worship. (WRO A1/250).

1867. Burial ground shown on sketch map of Quaker properties. (WRO 1699/104).

Marlborough. Meeting-house and burial ground.

1690. "The house of William Hitchcock" registered as a Quaker place of worship.

1702. Burial ground at Manton. Grid reference 172685.

1721. Purchase on behalf of Friends by John Cale and others from Thomas Higham of Marlborough, salesman, and his wife Mary of "messuage, tenement or dwelling house and buildings" in Marlborough High Street. This was rebuilt as a Friends meeting-house. (WRO 854/39)

1800. Meeting-house closed.

1812. Last burial.

1816. Meeting-house allowed to be used as a British School.

1831. Meeting-house sold.(WRO 854/39).

c.1834. Last Marlborough Friend, named Furnell, buried at Manton. (Diary of Norman Penney in library of Friends House, London).

1860. Burial ground leased for 60 years to Primitive Methodists to erect a chapel

1927. Burial ground sold.

1961. Regular meetings for worship re-started.

1985. Building in the Parade converted to a Friends Meeting House.

Melksham. Meeting-house and burial ground. *See* chapter 2.

Mere. Meeting-house only - no burial ground.

1701. Meeting-house "within the town" registered as a Quaker place of worship.

Pickwick. *See* Corsham.

Purton Stoke. Meeting-house and burial ground.

1690. "The House of Margaret Shannione" was registered as a Quaker place of worship.

1702. John Hall "of Woodstreet, London", gave a piece of land at Purton to build a meeting-house on.

1705 New meeting-house registered. There was a burial ground.

1799 Sale of meeting-house authorised by Quarterly Meeting.

1867. Burial ground shown on a sketch-map (WRO 1699/104) as still Quaker owned. But an undated gloss on page 66 of WRO 854/39 notes that "from the small value of the burial ground it was considered not worth the expense of conveying to new trustees"

1870. Property no longer listed as owned by Friends.

Salisbury. Meeting-house and burial ground.

1703. There was a meeting-house and burial ground.

1713. Registration of a "new-built" house in Gigant ("Gigging") Street.

1717. QM minutes refer to the "new meeting-house and burial ground" and to the old burial ground. Property later passed out of Quaker ownership. Quaker meetings for worship subsequently resumed in Rectory Road.

Shaw. Burial ground. *See* chapter 2.

Slaughterford. Meeting-house and burial ground. Grid reference 842738.

1656. George Fox ministered. (*Fox's Journal* - Nickalls ed - page 272).

1663. George Fox held "a very large meeting in a great barn". [*The Journal* page 450].

1673. Meeting-house and burial ground existed and George Fox ministered there.

1776. Meeting laid down. (*Journal of the Friends Historical Society* vol XLIV).

1806. Property had been sold (minute of Wilts MM held May 1806.) The building still stood in the 1920s (photos exist) but only ruins now remain.

Stanton. Burial ground.

1658. Acquired.

1800. Last interment.

1987. Sold.

Tytherton. Burial ground.

1659. Acquired. It was in the centre of the village.

1809. Last burial.

1930. Sold.

Warminster. Meeting-house and burial ground.

1663. Quakers acquired a plot of ground of 8 luggs at Laynes, Bugley, for use as a burial ground (WRO 854/34.

1690. "The House called the Meeting House" was registered as a Quaker place of worship.

1696. St Denys Church burial register records burial of Stephen Griffin at the Quakers Burying Place*.

1699. George Wansey buried at Lanes (or Laynes).

1719. Rebecca Kew alias Cox gave £20 towards building a meeting-house at Warminster. The money was not used.(WRO 1798/4).

1730. Ann Butler buried at Lanes*.

1795. George Gardiner, "the last Quaker in town", died*.

1851. Burial ground. Noted on page 76 of WRO 854/39 "this property is lost".

*According to *A History of Warminster* by the Reverend John J Daniell (1879). Daniell states that the meeting-house was in Common Close and afterwards became a malthouse. He describes the burial ground at Laynes, near Bugley, where he says, there had been Quaker burials within living memory, as being fifteen yards long and seven wide, enclosed within a low wall near a few trees beside the old pack-horse track from Bugley to Clay Hill.

There is now no longer any trace of the burial ground.

Westbury. Meeting-house and burial ground.

The only registration at Westbury was "the dwelling-house or hired house of James Matravers". [WRO A1/250]. But a meeting-house does seem to have existed. At WRO 854/44 is a postcard dated August 5 1894 from W Bott addressed to Norman Penney at Church Walk, Melksham, which states that "the meeting-house at Westbury is a brick building adjoining the churchyard and is now a stable. Burial ground is a narrow piece walled round with an entrance from the churchyard".

Whaddon (near Salisbury). Burial Ground.

1720. A minute of Quarterly Meeting in September refers to "writings" of the burial ground being placed in the Quarterly Meeting chest.

*   *   *

Frome (Somerset). Meeting-House and Burial Ground.

Close to the Wiltshire county border and grouped with Wiltshire Meetings was the meeting-house and burial ground at Frome. The first meeting-house was acquired in 1675.

In 1723, to judge by an "Account of the Meeting house expence etc" (expenditure of £96.12s.8d. and three farthings) the meeting-house had been substantially rebuilt or extended.

By 1866 meeting for worship had been discontinued. In that year the building was rented to the YMCA.

1867. Last burial (Deborah Lucas, in the small burial ground adjoining).

1956. Building sold to British Red Cross Society.

APPENDIX C

QUAKERS AT CORSHAM, PICKWICK AND DEVIZES

Corsham and Pickwick

In the early years of the movement Melksham Quakers met, together with Quakers from Corsham, discreetly at Shawhill.

In 1659 Corsham Friends acquired at Pickwick a plot of land for use as a burial-ground in addition to what they already possessed[1]. This additional land will have been bought to extend the burial ground at Pickwick. More land at Pickwick was acquired in 1708[2].

By 1690 they had a meeting-house at Corsham. In 1709 they built a new one there[3].

An active member of Corsham Meeting in those days was wealthy Caleb Dickinson (died 1728), of Monk's. A recorded minister, his house was used from time to time for monthly meetings and meetings of ministers. A faithful tithe-resister, the bailiffs regularly seized goods from him, in 1716, for example, plate worth £4.16s.4d. and subsequently hay and other agricultural produce. From April 1716 Quaker minister Thomas Story regularly stayed with the family when visiting Corsham while travelling "in the ministry". In 1731 Story stayed with Caleb's son Ezekiel who had inherited, recorded Story, "a great Estate, and he hardly of age: yet being of a singular good natural Temper, and very loving, and of an innocent Behaviour, temperate and prudent, Friends have great hopes he will do well; and many greatly desire he may."

In 1724 the Quaker school at Melksham under the excellent Thomas Bennet moved to Pickwick, thereby creating a potential new Quaker centre at no great distance from the existing one. In 1734, Thomas Bennet's premises were registered as a Quaker place of worship. (Registrants were Henry Sanger, John Neate junior, and Henry Seale junior)[4]. But meetings seem to have continued at Corsham until 1774 when, in exchange for the old meeting-house there, Charles Arnold erected a new one at Pickwick on ground adjacent to the burial ground[5].

Pickwick Meeting suffered the same fate as most other Wiltshire Quaker meetings. By the end of the eighteenth century it was moribund and in 1815, the Meeting no longer viable, the meeting-house was closed, such members as remained joining neighbouring Melksham Meeting. The school had faded away not long after the master's death in 1764. With the approval of Friends Bennet's son John had taken over from his father. By 1773, however, we find that he has become a weaver (though on his death in 1802 he was described as a yeoman). It seems likely that the school and Meeting were interdependent and went down together; the parents of Quaker children at a Quaker boarding-school would doubtless in those days have looked for a good Quaker Meeting within walking distance.

Devizes

Quakers in Devizes are known to have been meeting regularly for worship in their own meeting-house from the very earliest days of the movement. By virtue of a deed of 1647[6] they acquired "two tenements" evidently for use as a meeting place. The registration certificate required by the Toleration Act 1689 described this as being located "on the Greene". (The Green is still a Devizes location). In 1665 the Meeting leased land as a burial ground[7].

By the beginning of the eighteenth century they were strong enough in numbers and confidence to leave The Green for the town centre. On 6 July 1702 we find them reporting to Wiltshire Quarterly Meeting that their new Meeting house is nearly ready but that they have to find about £70 more over and above the proceeds from the sale of the old meeting house and the £250 which had been subscribed.

A registration certificate for the new meeting-house was granted on 10 July 1702, the registrants being William Coole. Joseph Bartlett and Stephen Jones. The certificate also included the dwelling-houses of William Coole and Joseph Bartlett as places of worship[8].

According to Edward and James Waylen, writing in the *Devizes Advertiser* in a series of articles between 3 May and 8 December 1877, under the heading 'Non-conformity in Devizes', in 1732 other churches in the town, including Anglicans, helped out when extra building work was needed.

As the eighteenth century wore on membership of the Society declined throughout the county and only Melksham Meeting remained strong, its numbers maintained by incorporation of remnants from nearby closed Meetings. Devizes Meeting shared in the decline but remained in being until 1826.

To judge by the Waylen articles, the Meeting in its declining years does not seem to have been conducted much like a Quaker one. It seems that in the last years one Abraham Gibbes had taken it upon himself to deliver a prepared sermon at every meeting for worship. His preaching drew large congregations, including Anglicans, and Abraham doubtless thought he was serving the Society. But his ill-judged effort hastened the end. When he moved to Nailsworth there was, not surprisingly, no Meeting member who wished to carry on in what had ceased to be a proper Quaker Meeting. Thereafter the building was leased to the Devizes Literary and Scientific Institution.

In 1840 the building was sold, but in 1858 bought back[10]. In that year Meetings for Worship were resumed but by 1874 membership had dwindled to two and in 1878 Monthly Meeting agreed to lay the Meeting down, the few remaining Devizes Friends being recommended to attend Melksham Meeting.[11]

The bulding was thereafter let for one or two evenings a week to temperance societies. In 1890 there seemed little likelihood of a revival of interest in regular meetings of the

Society in Devizes and a 21 year lease was granted to N Hise and E B Anslie acting on behalf of the Young Men's Christian Association with the proviso that Quaker Meetings could be held there if required. Between 1903 and 1906 an attempt was made to revive interest and regular Meetings for Worship were resumed with, at first, "usually six Friends and three Attenders present". But from March 1906 they were discontinued. By 1929 there seemed no prospect that the building would ever again be needed as a meeting-house and it was sold.

Half a century later Quakers came back to Devizes. The congregation at first comprised Friends living in or near Devizes but belonging to Bradford on Avon Meeting, itself a revival of the seventeenth century one which, like Devizes and most other Wiltshire Meetings had collapsed in the eighteenth century. At first Friends met for worship only. In the 1980s regular weekly meetings resumed, grew, and Devizes Meeting became once again established in its own right.

NOTES

1. WRO 854/34. They held land which had been acquired by copyhold dated 1641 from the Manor of Corsham (recorded in a "tabular statement" report to North Somerset and Wiltshire Monthly Meeting in 1879).

2. At Pickwick, in the Parish of Corsham, held of the Manor of Corsham by copy of Court Roll, the first being made 10 May 1708, "subject to a fine of one penny farthing at every Renewal of Lives or Trustees." This sum was originally three farthings, but by exchange a small parcel of land was added, entailing the additional halfpenny. (WRO 1798/4).

3. 10 December 1709. Registration of "a house lately erected on part of a close late in the possession of William Arnold". Registrants were John Hand, William Jeffries, John Butler, Richard Gowen, Thomas

Bayly, and John Flower. Wiltshire Record Society: *Meeting House Certificates 1689-1852* entry 177 on page 16. References are to Wilts Notes and Queries 5.550; 6,226; 6,230 and WRO A1/250.

4. WRO A1/250 and Wiltshire Record Society: *Wiltshire Meeting House Certificates 1689-1852* item 259.

5 Minute 3 of Wiltshire Quarterly Meeting held at Devizes 21 March 1774.

6. WRO 2269/48.

7. WRO 2269/49.

8. WRO A1/250 and Wiltshire Record Society: *Wiltshire Meeting House Certificates 1689-1852* no 129 on page 12.

9. WRO 854/39.

10. WRO 1798/4.

11. Minute of the North Somerset and Wiltshire Monthly Meeting October 1878.

Leaze Cottage, Watson's Court, Melksham was owned continuously by Melksham Quaker Meeting members from the seventeenth century until bought by Joseph Stratton, Melksham grocer and leading Methodist in 1874. (Photo by Dr. Gillian Cardy)

APPENDIX D

Leaze Cottage, 19 Watson's Court, Melksham
Leaze Cottage's links with Melksham Quakers spanned more than two centuries.

The Wiltshire Buildings Record report (by Pamela Slocombe) shows that Melksham Quakers owned the property continuously from the seventeenth century to the nineteenth. Though there is likely to be no more significance in this than that before the days of estate agents and local newspapers news of property for sale or to let travelled by word of mouth and that Melksham Quakers were a close-knit community within a community where news and gossip travelled fast, brief particulars from Mrs Slocombe's report may be worth noting here.

The earliest-known (seventeenth century) owner, Thomas Selfe, may have been an early Melksham Quaker. Many members of the Selfe family were. In 1697 Thomas sold the property, then two acres, to Henry Cox, butcher, and his wife Sarah. In 1699 Henry died and the property went to his three daughters, Mary, Sarah and Elizabeth. Mary married Quaker Thomas Shute, tallow-chandler. From 1720 Mary and Thomas occupied a third of the property and her sister Sarah and husband John Taylor, a butcher, occupied the rest, (which included Henry Cox's slaughterhouse), Elizabeth having sold her share to them.

Thomas Shute's first wife Mary having died, Thomas remarried in 1726. The Quaker register of marriages shows that in that year Thomas Shute, widower, married at Warminster Mary Cape, daughter of John Cape of Wellington, Somerset, and that Mary's parents were dead. In 1730 a son William was born. In 1731 Thomas's daughter Mary left Melksham for America. (Her certificate of removal — the document which Friends took with them when taking up residence elsewhere

—is listed in *Quaker arrivals at Philadelphia 1682-1750* (published by Ferris and Leach of Philadelphia in 1902).

In 1749 the property was sold to Quaker Dennis Newman (1720-1750), shopkeeper, as trustee for Quaker Paul Newman the Younger (1693-1760), Melksham clothier. In 1781 ownership passed from Paul Newman and his wife Margaret to Stephen Bourne, grocer and brandy merchant. Quaker family names continue to crop up in the deeds; in 1795 those of Matravers, Aaron Paradise (1753-1837), Dennis Newman and Mrs P Newman; and in 1800 that of William Newman of Beanacre. In 1817 we find Thomas Rose Newman involved as administrator of the estate of his father John Newman, who had been executor of Quaker benefactor Dennis Newman's will dated 26 September 1770.

In 1829, Quaker William Simpson, brushmaker, bought the property. Thomas Rose Newman, described in the documents as "not always sane" was then living at York (probably at The Retreat, the Quaker-run mental hospital there).

The Quaker connexion ceased in 1874 when Edward Simpson of Devizes, grocer, who had presumably inherited, sold to Joseph Stratton, Melksham grocer and leading Methodist, who had been living there from about 1850.

APPENDIX E

Henry Baron Smith

In 1902, in old age, Henry Baron Smith of Weston-super-Mare, wrote in an exercise book his recollections of Melksham Quaker Meeting as he had known it as a visitor in the latter half of the previous century. He called it "Melksham memories 1870 - 1892". [WRO 2269/33}.

Smith was married (1856) to Eliza, daughter of Thomas Ferris, schoolmaster and grocer of Melksham. Eliza had been governess to Mary and Elizabeth, the two daughters of William Simpson. The Simpsons lived at Leaze Cottage, Watson's Yard.

Smith first visited Melksham in 1859 and seems to have fallen in love with the town and the Quaker Meeting. Recollected in old age it wore "a halo of interesting and pleasing associations, brightened by the memories of good and worthy Friends". In the Melksham Quaker Meeting there seemed to prevail "a truly Christian brotherly feeling". Frequently mentioned in connexion with local good works were members of the Fowler family, William Matravers, George Kirby, Isaac Lloyd and William and Robert Simpson. "The meeting-house was well filled".

Smith recalls The Lawn, the girls' boarding school run by Quaker Emma Sturge and her daughters. (It was in Devizes Road, in the neighbourhood known as The Spa; earlier his father-in-law Thomas Ferris had conducted a school at the same premises). Near it stood a "neat little cottage" occupied by Quaker Elizabeth Barling, a widow "whose son had met with an early death". (The census return for 1861 records that Elizabeth Barling, aged 56, widow, was an "annuitant", living in Spa Road, with one servant.In 1875, according to Kellys Directory, she was living at Spero Lodge).

"A little further down on the same side was Maria Simpson's". Maria had been handicapped from childhood, having injured her spine as the result of falling down the stairs. Robert and Emma Simpson lived there till Emma's death. (1881 census return lists the household two entries away from The Lawn and that in that year Emma was eighty years old). The house was a "most luxurious and hospitable hostel for many a wayfarer on worthy errand bent. For some years Elizabeth Jeffrey and daughter occupied rooms therein". It was "a favourite rendezvous for Friends".

Smith tells us that Henry Simpson later acquired the house and carried on his ironmongery business there. (At the 1881 census the Simpson household was still in the High Street. It comprised Henry aged 44, his wife Caroline aged 38, five daughters and one domestic servant. Employed in the business were eight men and seven boys. From North Somerset and Wiltshire Monthly Meeting minutes for September 1883 we learn that the business has failed and Henry is heavily in debt. For this he is severely censured).

Rachel Fowler occupied "quite a long range of house...where wealthy and distinguished, as well as the poor and destitute found fitting entertainment and relief. The focus of benevolence that emanated from this quarter" wrote Smith, "will long be remembered".

The Mallinson and the Matravers families lived near by. (Fowler and Mallinson had earlier on been in business together in Bank Street as tea dealers and hop merchants). Matravers carried on a cloth factory. "Their cloth had a good name. It was almost too good for the market". This will have been William and John Howard Matravers, who set up in Melksham in 1862 when their factory at Westbury burnt down. The firm closed in 1888; (*see* Rogers: *Wiltshire and Somerset Woollen Mills* published 1976 by Pasold Research Fund Ltd). The 1871 census return shows that John Howard Matravers, aged 44, and his wife Mary, aged 38 lived in Bath Road and that John was a woollen manufacturer employing 110 persons; and that another member of the Matravers family, Caroline, widow of a woollen manufacturer (probably William, John's partner), aged 70, was living at Avon Bridge with unmarried daughter Mary, aged 41, married daughter Lucy Stiles, aged 29 and her husband Ernest Awdry Stiles, aged 30 and granddaughter Maud aged 10.

Another Matravers, Thomas, aged 40, lived with his wife Mary, aged 30, in the Market Place with their sons Percy, aged ten, and William, aged four, and daughters Mary, aged seven and Mabel aged one. He was a clock manufacturer.

Smith recorded that between 1874 when, "with the approval and encouragement of local Friends", he began to make frequent visits to Melksham Friends Meeting, up to 1892, he visited 62 times. On week-end visits he would travel by train from Weston-super-Mare, where he was a teacher, returning on Monday morning to arrive in time to take his first class.

It is clear from Smith's account that though by now the Melksham Meeting was much diminished in numbers and scope it was still a viable worshipping community. He remembered the names of some of the congregation, which included numerous Simpsons; Rachel Fowler and her visitors; frequent visits by "R N Fowler of Corsham" (though Sir Robert Fowler, as we have seen, had left the Society of Friends to become a member of the Church of England, it is clear from this that he had not cut himself off completely from Friends); the Matravers family; Mrs Styles — that would be the above-mentioned Lucy Stiles; Emma Sturge and pupils; the Selman family — William Robert Selman was a tailor in Lowbourne (earlier Canon Square) and Registering Officer for Friends; Arthur Brereton ("who married Edith Simpson"); William Guye; Thomas Webb and family; R Paradise; John Peters and wife; A Rosling "at the iron works"; Richards "from the tollgate"; Martin "the aged"; "a railway porter"; and M A Chapple. There were others whose names he could not remember.

After Meeting for Worship Smith would often call at the

home of Philip Phelps and discuss with his invalid daughter what had been said. He enjoyed the Phelps family Bible reading. "Philip Phelps's manner was so impressive and reverent when engaged in prayer, he was a truly good man!". (The 1881 census return shows that Philip Phelps, widower, then aged 74, was living in Market Place with daughters Fanny aged 43, Elizabeth aged 39 and Jane Rose aged 36, also his sister-in-law Francis Anne Phene aged 60 and two aunts. Phelps was Clerk to the Income Tax Commissioners, Clerk to the Board of Guardians of the Melksham Union, Land Agent and Superintendent Registrar).

Of those named by Smith many were active in town affairs. Of the 22 Town Commissioners listed in Kellys Directory for 1875 no less than four were Quakers — John Howard Matravers, Thomas Matravers, Philip Phelps and Henry Simpson. Thomas Matravers was also honorary secretary of the Cottage Hospital in Lowbourne.

APPENDIX F

To Mary from her Samuel (Samuel Rutty 1695-1762, see page 69)

Cherished (and kept safe from the rats!) by his beloved Mary and discovered 200 years later in the attic of the old mill-house at Gillingham, Dorset, were four affectionate letters from Samuel, one (29 May 1732) while Mary was away, evidently staying with relatives, at Taunton; two the following year (17 and 22 May) while Samuel was away attending London Yearly Meeting and taking the opportunity while he was in town to do a little business there; and one written (19 June 1735) while Mary was away at Fordingbridge, again having a little holiday with relatives.

The letters are in the possession of the Shaftesbury and District Historical Society and Walter Birmingham kindly had copies made for me. They are commonplace enough in their content — much the sort of thing, part domestic and business affairs and part affectionate greetings, that over the centuries folk have written to their nearest and dearest. But they help to make what would otherwise be merely names on a page into something just a little more.

The letter written to Mary on holiday at Taunton in May 1732 reports that the children are well. Son Jonathan (aged 9) continues at the Quaker school at Pickwick. Business is good but he is finding it hard going without her help, though she must not let the thought of that spoil her holiday. Nevertheless will she let him know what her plans are as to when she intends to return... He has not been well and puts it down to cider-drinking (one assumes, as he warns Mary to take care, that it was the quality of the drink rather than the amount drunk). There is a PS stating that "Sir Philip is not yet come". (Sir Philip's expected visit evidently signifies important business for Samuel connected in some way with neighbouring village Steeple Ashton).

The one written on Thursday 17 May 1733 from Samuel to Mary at Melksham is in reply to one from her (not, alas, extant). Samuel is up for London Yearly Meeting and will stay on to attend to private business when it is over. Meanwhile Yearly Meeting is in full swing and is not expected to end before Saturday afternoon (19th). Samuel expects his own business matters to be settled by the following Wednesday (23rd). He also again has something to transact with "Sir Philip" who is expected in London from Suffolk about the 26th and he seeks Mary's advice whether he shall "stay it out until Sir Philip comes" or come away as soon as what he calls his "own business" is done. (The business with "Sir Philip" is in some way connected with James Tayler and Steeple Ashton).

The letter written on Tuesday 22 May is again in reply to one from Mary. Yearly Meeting, which went well, with large and good meetings, ended Saturday night. He has despatched that afternoon a load of goods for William Bryan, the Overton waggoner to deliver to Melksham the following Saturday or Monday. "Sir Philip" arrived in London the previous day. Samuel has spent the whole day with him and intends to settle his accounts with him before he leaves town. Mary is to see that George Dark keeps separate the account for the last "spinning-house day" from the one for the work he brings home while Samuel is still away, which is to wait until he gets back. (Spinning was not done "in-house" by clothiers but by independent weavers). He ends with loving assurance that neither time nor distance can diminish his affection for her.

In the summer of 1735 Mary is again away staying with their relations, this time at Fordingbridge, and Samuel is longing for her return. On 19 June 1735 he sends his man Peter with a letter replying to hers urging her to return at the week-end and not allow herself to be persuaded to stay longer. If she feels that the ride back to Melksham in one day will be too much for her she is to leave on Friday afternoon and stay the night at Salisbury. He concludes again with patently sincere affection; her absence has reminded him that death will part them one day and that they must make the most of their life on earth together. (In the event, Mary died two years later).

APPENDIX G

(i) 10 King Street (on the north side of the meeting-house)
Melksham Quakers bought the house in 1819 from the trustees of John Whale, of Melksham of whom Robert Fowler was one, for £205.16s.6d. the money being put up by Robert Fowler, William Matravers and Mary Jeffry. The property comprised a dwelling-house with outhouse, garden and orchard adjoining "containing by estimate two acres". The property was bought as an investment, the rents to be used for repairs to the meeting house, education, apprentice fees, marriage portions, attending meetings and so on. (WRO 1798/4)

Deeds dated 28 and 29 September 1809 in the Wiltshire Record Office Quaker Collection, show that John Whale of Melksham, gentleman — described elsewhere as yeoman — bought it from the trustees of a marriage settlement made in 1794 by John Awdry in respect of the marriage of his eldest son John, of Notton, Wilts, to Jane Bigg, daughter of Lovelace Bigg Wither.

The house was sold in 1958.

(ii) 16 King Street (on the south side of the meeting-house)
This was acquired by Melksham Quakers in 1811 for £380. They bought it as an investment to service thirteen small charitable trusts created since 1696.

When they bought it the house had been built within the past few years, probably in or a little before 1808, on a site of a house which had a long history of Quaker ownership. In the 1680s it had belonged to Quaker John Hancock, who had inherited it from his father Nathaniel. John Hancock's executor was Quaker Simon Shewring, yeoman (elsewhere described as surgeon), of Canhold, Melksham. He sold it on a 958 year lease to John Barrow "joyner" and thereafter the property was owned successively by Jane Barrow, John's widow (from 1715 to 1731) who left it to Nicholas Twining (or Twinny) of Seend, butcher (from 1721 to 1742) who sold to Edward Knight of Newtown, Melksham, clothworker (died 1806). Mary Flower, born Knight, widow, Edward Knight's niece and administratrix had the new house built. She sold it in 1808 to Isaac Ashley, yeoman, of Semington who sold it to Melksham Friends.

It was sold, with the old meeting-house, in 1958.

APPENDIX H

TRUSTEES NAMED IN DEEDS

The following lists of names of trustees may be helpful to genealogists and family historians. I took them from such Quaker deeds and documents in the Wiltshire Record Office as were connected with Melksham Quakers. They are by no means exhaustive and serve mainly as an example of what might be discovered by a family historian with a Quaker in the family tree. There are a number of bundles of deeds and documents relating to Quaker property in Wiltshire going back to the mid-seventeenth century and most of them contain names, occupations and residence of Quaker trustees. Besides this primary material there are abstracts and property records made at various dates notably at WRO 854/34, WRO 854/ 37, WRO 854/39, WRO 1699/105 and WRO 1798/4.

Meeting-house and burial ground at Melksham:

1698

Beaven, Thomas the Younger	Melksham	clothier
Clark, John	Bradford on Avon	chymist
Gingall Thomas	Corsham	yeoman
Hodges, John	Warminster	maltster
Hull, Joseph	Frankleigh	clothier
Jefferys, John	Melksham	schoolmaster
Poulsome, Thomas	Purlpit	yeoman
Rutty, John	Melksham	maltster
Sanger, Henry	Melksham	clothier
Shewring, Simon	Melksham	surgeon
Smith, William	Whitley, Melksham	maltster

1705

Axford, Isaac	Stoke	yeoman
Bayley, Thomas	Pickwick	yeoman
Beaven, Thomas	Melksham	clothier
Clark, John	Bradford on Avon	chymist
Cole, Joseph	Calne	serge-maker
Cook, Roger the Younger	Chippenham	clothier
Gerrish, Thomas the Younger	Bromham	yeoman
Gouldney, Adam	Chippenham	yeoman
Grant, George	Bradford on Avon	clothier
Gye, John	Market Lavington	maltster
Hunt, Henry the Younger,	Bishop's Cannings	yeoman
Matravers, James	Westbury	linen draper
Hodges, John	Warminster	maltster
Hudden, John	Melksham	shearman
Jefferies, John	Corsham	schoolmaster
Jefferies, William	Charlcut	serge-maker
Newman, Paul	Melksham	tailor
Rutty, John	Melksham	shopkeeper
Self, Isaac the Younger	Market Lavington	cardmaker
Shewring, Simon	Melksham	surgeon
Smith, William	Whitley, Melksham	maltster
Street, Benjamin the Younger	Devizes	clothier
Street, John the Younger	Calne	serge-maker
Treeland, Thomas	Bratton	cordwainer
Tyler, Jonathan	Bradford on Avon	dyer
Walker, William	Brinkworth	yeoman
Young, Thomas, son of David	Brinkworth	yeoman

1734

Beaven, Thomas	late of Melksham now of Bristol	gentleman
Beaven, Thomas the Younger	Melksham	clothier

Dickson, Thomas	Turley	clothier
Dickinson, Ezekiel	Corsham	gentleman
Dye, Joseph, son of Edward, deceased	Lavington	maltster
Furnell, Isaac the Younger	Marlborough	maltster
Hull, Joseph	Frankleigh	clothier
Hull, Thomas	Frankleigh	clothier
Jefferys, John	late of Melksham now of London	schoolmaster
Moore, James	Melksham	clothier
Neat, Thomas	Calne	drugget-maker
Rose, Charles	Devizes	maltster
Sanger, Henry	Warminster	maltster
Sanger, Samuel	Melksham	clothier
Tyler, Charles	Bradford on Avon	clothier

1777

Beaven, John, son of Thomas Granton
Beaven, Samuel, son of Thomas Melksham
Beaven, Thomas the Younger Melksham
(John, Samuel and Thomas were sons of Thomas "late of Melksham now of Granton, gentleman")

Bennet. John	Pickwick	gentleman
Bennet, Thomas	Pickwick	gentleman
Dickinson, Ezekiel	Bowden Hill, Lacock	esquire
Fowler, Robert	Melksham	grocer
Fowler, Thomas	Melksham	grocer
Hipsley, Samuel	Melksham	baker
Hipsley, Samuel the Younger	Melksham	baker
Jefferys, Robert	Melksham	maltster
Jefferys, Robert the Younger son of Robert	Melksham	
Jefferys, Thomas	Melksham	

Jefferys, Edward	Melksham	
Jefferys, Edward the Younger	Melksham	
son of Edward		
Matravers, John	Westbury	grocer
Matravers, William	Westbury	grocer
Moore, James	late New Sarum, gentleman	
	now Granton, Somerset	
Moxham, Benjamin	Melksham	baker
Moxham, Paul	Melksham	baker
Riley, John the Younger	Wilton	grocer
Riley, Thomas the Younger	Whitley	baker
son of Thomas of Whitley		
Sanger, Samuel	Melksham	clothier
Smith, William	Bromham	yeoman
Smith, William the Younger	Bromham	yeoman
Smith, Thomas	Bromham	yeoman
Smith, Clare	Bromham	baker
Sturge, Thomas	New Sarum	fellmonger

Melksham burial-ground

1790

Beaven, Thomas	Grinton (?Granton)	
	Somerset	gentleman
Bennet, John	Pickwick	gentleman
Bennet, Thomas	Pickwick	gentleman
Hipsley, Samuel	Melksham	baker
Jefferys, Robert	Melksham	mealman
Jefferys, Edward	Melksham	
Jefferys, Edward the Younger		
son of Edward	Melksham	
Jefferys, Thomas		
son of Robert	Melksham	

Fowler, Robert	Melksham	merchant
Matravers, John	Westbury	banker
Matravers, William	Westbury	banker
Moxham, Benjamin	Melksham	baker
Moxham, Paul	Bristol	baker
Riley, John	Devizes	baker
Smith,Clare	City of London	baker
Smith, William	Bromham	yeoman
Sturge, Thomas	Southwark	

Dwelling-house on south side of Friends meeting-house (16 King Street)

1811

Dent, David	Melksham	clothier
Fowler, John	Melksham	wine merchant
Fowler, Thomas	Melksham	farmer
Jefferys, Thomas	Melksham	mealman
Matravers, John	Westbury	clothier
Moxham, John	Melksham	ironmonger
Paull, Richard	Melksham	mealman

1813

Allis, Thomas	Tewkesbury	hosier
Brown, Thomas Crowther and Robert Jefferys, sons of Thomas, wine merchant		
Capper, Samuel	Potterne Farm	yeoman
Gayner, John	Filton, Glos	yeoman
Gilkes, Benjamin Gilbert	Nailsworth	schoolmaster
Gundry, William	Calne	grocer
Hartland Nathaniel the Younger	Tewkesbury	mealman

Matravers, William
    the Younger   Westbury   clothier

Padbury, William	Ashton Keynes, Glos	yeoman

Sanger, Mildred, son of John Sanger, ironmonger
Sturge, Thomas Marshall, son of Joseph Sturge of Olveston, yeoman

Thomas, Alfred	West Ashton	yeoman
Wilkins, Henry	Cirencester	woolstapler
Wilkins, John the Younger	Cirencester	woolstapler

Dwelling-house on north side of the meeting-house (10 King Street)

1813

Fowler, Robert	Melksham	gentleman
Gundry, Joseph	Calne	woolstapler
Jefferys, Mary	Melksham	spinster
Matravers, John	Westbury	clothier
Matravers, William	Westbury	clothier
Nalder, Thomas	Melksham	gentleman

1819

Allis, Thomas	Tewkesbury	yeoman
Allis, Haggar	Tewkesbury	ironmonger
Bowley, David	Cirencester	mealman
Bowley, William Crotch	Cirencester	mealman
Brewin, Robert, son of John	Cirencester	coal merchant
Brown, Thomas Crowther	Cirencester	wine merchant
Brown, Joshua son of		
Thomas the Elder	Cirencester	
Dent, David	Melksham	clothier
Fowler, John	Melksham	wine merchant
Fowler, Robert	Melksham	gentleman

Fowler, Robert the Younger Melksham
Fowler, Thomas   Melksham   farmer
Fry, Francis and Joseph, sons of Joseph of Frenchay, gentleman
Gayner, John   Filton, Glos   yeoman
Gundry, Joseph   Calne   woolstapler
Gundry, Joseph the Younger
  son of Joseph   Calne
Gundry, William, son of
  Joseph   Calne
Gundry, William   Calne   grocer
Jefferys, Edward son of
  Thomas   Melksham
Jefferys, Mary   Melksham   spinster
Jefferys, Robert   Cirencester   wine merchant
Jefferys, Robert son of
  Thomas   Melksham
Jefferys, Samuel, son of
  Thomas   Melksham
Jefferys, Thomas   Melksham   mealman
Matravers, William   Westbury   clothier
Paull, Richard   Melksham   mealman
Powell, John, son of William Powell the Younger of Potterne
Park,   yeoman
Simpson, William   Melksham   brushmaker
Sturge, Thomas Marshall   Olveston   woolstapler
Tucket, Philip Debel and Francis, sons of Philip Debel Tucket,
late of Frenchay, gentleman, deceased

Burial-ground and other property in Melksham and Bromham

1870
Allis, Thomas   Osbaldwicks, Yorks
                  formerly Tewkesbury gentleman

Bobbett, John Winter the Younger	Bristol	baker
Brisson, Alfred	Bristol	brushmaker
Brown, Edgar Marriage	Weston-super-Mare	grocer
Brown, Thomas Crowther	Cirencester	wine merchant
Fry, David	Bristol	starch-manufacturer
Fry, Lewis	Bristol	solicitor
Fry, Walter Gawen	Bristol	accountant
Gayner, John	Almondsbury	yeoman
Gayner, William	Filton	yeoman
Grace, Alexander	Bristol	mealman
Grace, James and Henry	Bristol	house agents
Hunt, Theodore	Bristol	leather factor

Jefferys, Edward and John Henry sons of Samuel Alexander
Jefferys, of Melksham, gentleman

Simpson, Edward	Devizes	grocer
Simpson, Henry	Melksham	ironmonger
Sturge, William	Chipping Sodbury formerly Kemble	gentleman
Tanner, James	Cheddar	paper manufacturer
Thompson, Lewis	Bridgewater	cheese factor
Clark, William Stephens	Street	shoe manufacturer
Tuckett, Francis Fox	Frenchay	leather factor

Chippenham meeting-house

1778

Fowler, Robert	Melksham	shopkeeper
Hipsley, Samuel the Elder	Melksham	baker
Hipsley, Samuel the Younger	Melksham	baker
Jeffrys, Edward the Elder	Melksham	mealman
Jeffrys, Edward the Younger	Melksham	mealman
Jeffrys, Robert the Elder	Melksham	mealman

Jeffrys, Robert the Younger	Melksham	mealman
Moore, James	late of Melksham now of Salisbury	gentleman
Moxham, John	Melksham	bellows-maker
Moxham, Paul	Melksham	baker
Sanger, Samuel	Melksham	clothier
Yerbury, Joseph	Melksham	clothier

Cottage adjoining Chippenham meeting-house

1805

Fowler, John, son of Robert	Melksham	
Fowler, Robert the Elder	Melksham	brandy merchant
Fowler, Thomas, son of Robert	Melksham	
Moxham, Benjamin	Melksham	baker
Neate, Samuel	Chippenham	esquire
Paul, Richard, son of Wiliam	Melksham	
Paul, Jefferys, son of William	Melksham	
Paul, William	Melksham	clothier

Stanton burial-ground

1784

Hipsley, Samuel	Melksham	baker
Hipsley, Samuel, son of Samuel	Melksham	
Hipsley, Richard, son of Samuel	Melksham	

168

Jefferys, Robert	Melksham	mealman
Jefferys, Thomas, son of Robert	Melksham	
Jefferys, Edward the Younger	Melksham	
Matravers, John	Westbury	mercer
Matravers, William	Westbury	plate-maker
Moxham, Benjamin	Melksham	baker
Moxham, John the Younger	Melksham	bellows-maker

Benjamin Street and Joseph Bartlett's Charity: land at Bulkington

1825

Beaven, Thomas	Bruton, Somerset	gentleman
Bowley, William Crotch	Cirencester	mealman
Bowley, Samuel	Cirencester	mealman
Brewin, John	Cirencester	coal merchant
Brewin, Thomas son of John	Cirencester	
Brown, Thomas Crowther	Cirencester	wine merchant
Brown, Robert Jefferys	Cirencester	woolstapler
Brown, Joshua, son of Edward	Cirencester	wine merchant
Fewster, Anthony Rogers	Horsley, Glos	mealman
Fowler, Robert	Melksham	wine merchant

Fowler, Thomas, John and Robert the Younger, sons of Robert
Fry, Joseph and Francis, sons of Joseph Storrs Fry, chocolate-maker of Frenchay,Glos

Gayner, John	Filton, Glos	yeoman
Gundry, Joseph Fry	Calne	woolstapler

Gundry, Joseph and William, sons of Joseph Fry Gundry

Gundry, William	Calne	gentleman
Harland, John Allis	Tewkesbury	banker

Hunt, Josiah and James the Younger, sons of James Hunt, farmer of Almondsbury

Jefferies, Thomas	Melksham	mealman
Jefferies, Samuel Alexander and Edward, sons of Thomas		
Matravers,William	Melksham	clothier
Moxham, Benjamin	Bristol	baker
Norton, William	Melksham	grocer
Paull. Richard	Melksham	mealman
Powell, William	Melksham	gentleman
Simpson, Robert	Melksham	ironmonger
Simpson, Wiliam	Melksham	brushmaker
Smith, Clare	Crofton nr Gt Bedwin	
Tuckett, Philip Debell	Frenchay	woolstapler

Properties at Bradford on Avon, Calne, Devizes, Marlborough, Preshute and Melksham

1826

Beaven, Thomas	Granton, Somerset	gentleman
Fowler, Thomas, eldest son of Robert Fowler of Melksham, wine merchant deceased	Broad Street, London	banker
Fry, Joseph Storrs	Frenchay	chocolate-maker
Matravers, William	Westbury	clothier

[who "signed by mark, having lost the use of his arm by paralysis"]

Moxham, Benjamin	Bristol	baker
Riley, Thomas	?	?
Sargent, Isaac	Paddington, Middx	accountant

Gift of £450 from the will (1812) of John Matravers of Westbury, clothier.

1880

Bowly, William	Cirencester	miller
Brown, Alfred	Gloucester	merchant
Sessions, Frederick	Gloucester	brickmaker
Simpson, Edward Theobald	Devizes	grocer
Simpson, Henry	Melksham	ironmonger
Theobald, Alfred Ernest	Bath	grocer
West, Edward the Younger	Congresbury	miller

Witnesses to signatures at Monthly Meeting held at Yatton 14 April 1880:-

Joseph Theobald, grocer, of 25 Stall Street, Bath
Robert Kingston Willmott, grocer, Congresbury
George Clark Gobey, accountant, 2 Hampden Villas, Cromwell Street, Gloucester.

Friends Burial Ground near Hillworth Road, Devizes. Trustees who sold in 1905 to Alexander Grant Meek (WRO 2269/49):

Ashby, Edmund	Sidcot School Somerset	schoolmaster
Brereton, Arthur Frederick	Ashford, Kent	excise officer
Brown, Arthur Edgar	Holmcott Weston-super-Mare	gentleman
Brown, Wilfred Marriage	Brantholme Weston-super-Mare	gentleman
Brown, Charles JP Lycroft	Weston-super-Mare	gentleman
Burchem, Charles	Fairlea, Sidcot	gentleman
Burchem, Charles Henry	Tethorpe, Caerleon, Monmouth	gentleman

Carter, George Baker	Somerton, Somerset	gentleman
Clark, Henry Robert	Sidcot School Somerset	schoolmaster
Hadfield, Samuel	Arnos Vale, Bristol	gentleman
Knight, Francis Arnold Wintrath Winscombe		gentleman
Langmaid, William Edward	Birkdale, Southport, Chester	gentleman
Lidbetter, Thomas	Halifax, Yorks	gentleman
Sturge, Edward Young	Chestnut Bank, Fritchley, Derby	gentleman
Sturge, Francis Lionel Player	Bootham School York	gentleman
Simpson, Edward Theobald	Devizes	grocer
Smith, Henry Baron	Southside House Weston-super-Mare	gentleman
Theobald, Alfred Ernest	Stall Street, Bath	grocer
Wedmore, Samuel	The Retreat, York	gentleman
Wood, Walter James	Newport, Mon	gentleman

BIBLIOGRAPHY

Works useful for further reference include:

1. History

The beginnings of Quakerism: William C Braithwaite. Sessions 1981

The Second Period of Quakerism: William C Braithwaite. Sessions 1979.

The Later Periods of Quakerism: Rufus Jones. Macmillan 1921.

Quaker Encounters, in three volumes: John Ormerod Greenwood. Sessions 1977.

The early History of the Society of Friends in Bristol and Somersetshire: William Tanner. 1858.

The Victoria County History, Wiltshire, vol VII.

The Story of the Steam Plough Works: Michael R Lane. Northgate Publishing Co Ltd.

Portrait in Grey: John Punshon. Quaker Home Service 1984.

Quakers in Science and Industry: Arthur Raistrick. David and Charles 1950.

The Quaker Lloyds in the Industrial Revolution: Humphrey Lloyd.

2. Biography

The Life of Sir Robert Fowler: John Stephen Flynn. 1893.

A Memoir of Richard Reynolds: Hannah Mary Rathbone 1852.

3. Source and reference material

The Journal of George Fox, edited by John L Nickalls. Cambridge University Press. 1952).

Christian Faith and Practice in the Experience of the Society of Friends (Friends House, London 1966).

A Collection of the Sufferings of the People called Quakers: Joseph Besse. London. 1753.

Wiltshire Meeting House Certificates 1689-1852: John Chandler, Wiltshire Record Society. 1985.

The Dictionary of National Biography.

Unpublished sources

The Fowler Hamily History. Privately printed for circulation among members of the family in 1899. Xerox copy available in Melksham Public Library.

A Memoir of Rachel Fowler. Privately printed in 1838 for circulation among members of the family. Copy in library of Woodbrooke College, Selly Oak, Birmingham.

A Dictionary of Quaker Biography. Unpublished. May be consulted in the library of Friends House, London.

INDEX OF NAMES
(See also Appendix H)

GENERAL INDEX.

(Illustrations are in bold type)

I am happy to be able to round off my account of the rise and decline of Quakerism in Wiltshire, as reflected in this account of Melksham Meeting, with encouraging news from neighbouring Devizes.

As I go to press, Devizes Quakers, who for the past ten years or so have been worshipping in private homes or rented premises, are about to occupy their new premises at Sussex Wharf. Although they have much to do before the new meeting-house can achieve its full potential as a Quaker centre they have, at last, once again somewhere to call their own where, I know, all worshippers will be welcome.

I wish them godspeed.

H.F.